EXECUTIVE SUPPORT FOR
WHEN NOT IF: A CEO'S GUIDE TO OVERCOMING ADVERSITY

The thought of ending up bankrupt, divorced, and imprisoned after living a life based on doing the right thing is untenable. Unfortunately, it is the life Jeff Martinovich lived and has captured in his book, *When Not If: A CEO's Guide to Overcoming Adversity*, along with an impossible comeback! Jeff's riveting story forces you to reassess your view of our systems and ponder if you would have the resilience to continue to survive? Be ready to have your core beliefs challenged!

—Paul Meyer
CEO, 55 Industries, LLC

An exceptional and enlightening book showcasing the remarkable journey of a business maverick who turned adversity into triumph. A compelling blend of practical business advice and profound life lessons. A true testament to the power of resilience and personal growth. Highly recommended!

—Kevin Cadieux
VP, Vertafore

Jeff amazes me with his acumen, diligence, and good nature in business, life, and his writing. This book provides a tremendous number of business actionable takeaways, as well as a unique view of a judicial system that is only as good as the people that operate within it.

—Frank Hunt
COO, Combat Bound

In over fifteen years of knowing Jeff Martinovich, both professionally and personally, I've had the privilege of witnessing his remarkable journey firsthand—from soaring heights to profound depths and back again. Jeff's *When Not If* isn't just a book; it's a raw, transparent testimony of leadership, resilience, and the indomitable spirit of the human soul. The authenticity with which Jeff acknowledges his flaws, takes ownership, and extracts profound insights is both admirable and deeply instructive. This book is a beacon for leaders navigating the treacherous waters of decision-making in volatile times. It serves as a stark reminder that true leadership is not about perpetual ascendancy but the ability to rise, reinvent, and redefine oneself amidst adversity. I wholeheartedly recommend *When Not If* to anyone who wishes to elevate their leadership journey by embracing both their triumphs and their trials.

—Ken Monroe
CEO, Background Investigation Bureau

WHEN

NOT IF

JEFF MARTINOVICH & JOHN KADOR

WHEN

NOT IF

A CEO'S GUIDE TO
OVERCOMING
ADVERSITY

Forbes | Books

Published by Forbes Books, Charleston, South Carolina.
An imprint of Advantage Media Group.

Forbes Books is a registered trademark, and the Forbes Books colophon is a trademark of Forbes Media, LLC.

Printed in the United States of America.

10 9 8 7 6 5 4 3 2 1

ISBN: 979-8-88750-209-0 (Hardcover)
ISBN: 979-8-88750-210-6 (eBook)

Library of Congress Control Number: 2023913690

Cover design by Analisa Smith.
Layout design by Megan Elger.

This custom publication is intended to provide accurate information and the opinions of the author in regard to the subject matter covered. It is sold with the understanding that the publisher, Forbes Books, is not engaged in rendering legal, financial, or professional services of any kind. If legal advice or other expert assistance is required, the reader is advised to seek the services of a competent professional.

Since 1917, Forbes has remained steadfast in its mission to serve as the defining voice of entrepreneurial capitalism. Forbes Books, launched in 2016 through a partnership with Advantage Media, furthers that aim by helping business and thought leaders bring their stories, passion, and knowledge to the forefront in custom books. Opinions expressed by Forbes Books authors are their own. To be considered for publication, please visit **books.Forbes.com**.

With inexpressible love and gratitude to
Ashleigh, Cole, Carleigh, and Mom for proving to me
the strength of family … and incredible gratitude to
Kevin, Brian, and Paul for teaching me the power of true friendship.

CONTENTS

AUTHOR'S NOTE

THESE FACTS AND PARTICULARS, as well as the adventures and misadventures that constitute this account, are verifiably accurate. I have the dubious distinction of having the last fifteen years of my life well documented on the federal record. I drew on that record—available to any reader who chooses to check any particular detail—to confirm the dates, names, and quotations that support this chronicle. Only in the case of a few anecdotes about some remarkable people I came to know on this journey have I used only their first names with respect for their privacy.

From the first day of this challenging experience, I committed to ensuring, above all, that every motion, petition, and letter filed were 100 percent accurate, without exaggeration, the whole truth and nothing but the truth, as I knew one misstep would invalidate any possible remaining credibility in this battle for my life. After losing everything, I knew the truth was the only foundation my fragile existence could stand upon—without truth, all would be lost.

Finally, I want to express my sincere regret for what my employees, shareholders, and family went through. The constraints of the legal system never allowed for authentic communications, apologies, and actions to remedy these failures sooner than later. As this book is one step in a restorative journey, I am hopeful I may be, finally, able to write a positive final chapter for everyone affected by these events. While this book is written from my personal vantage point, I pray the miraculous events now unfolding also repair and restore the lives of so many others. This is my mission.

ADVERSITY DOESN'T BUILD CHARACTER, IT REVEALS IT

IMAGINE FOR A MOMENT you have achieved a relatively impressive level of success leading and growing a business. Let's say you run a billion-dollar investment fund. Now imagine everything you possess is taken from you: your beautiful home, your Mercedes sedan, your favorite sports car, perhaps your fine wine from Napa and Bordeaux, maybe a deal watch or two, a boat or even a jet over at the local airport! Oh, and every dollar in all of your bank accounts, personal and business, is zeroed out. Everything you now and have ever possessed is gone.

Simultaneously, your marriage of nearly twenty years crumbles and divorce proceedings begin. Your children are upset, confused, and traumatized by events they do not understand. Your business associates turn on you or ignore you, and some of your friends (but thankfully not all) delete you from their iPhone contacts to ensure they are not tainted by association.

Now add one more brushstroke to this painting. Imagine you are charged with multiple felonies and threatened with a decade or longer prison sentence *without having committed any crime*!

How would you react, after the disbelief, anger, and various stages of grief?

In the short term, you'd have some decisions to make pretty quickly. Would you, if you honestly felt you broke no law, accept a plea deal? Would you, in open court, swear under oath that you broke the law in exchange for a substantially reduced prison sentence? Or would you take a stand knowing that the government, once they set their sights on you, rarely loses?

Before you answer, allow me to tell you about two successful executives, both well known to me, who were targeted by prosecutors and faced years of federal investigation. One escaped prosecution, while Jeffrey Martinovich, the author of this book, didn't fare so well. He was indicted and sentenced to fourteen years in federal prison, and as I write this, Jeff is finishing up his term in home detention wearing an ankle monitor. Unfortunately, it no longer seems far-fetched to me that CEOs and senior executives need to have a game plan in case the government comes calling . . . *whether or not any crime has been committed.*

Tony's Story

As fellow graduates of the US Air Force Academy, I had known Tony for more than thirty years, and I knew he was a person of character. Both of us led businesses in the defense sector, and we sometimes partnered on programs. When his attorneys contacted me saying they needed help understanding our business relationships, I was curious what that might be about.

Upon checking in, Tony assured me the request was legitimate and that the attorneys were acting on his instructions. "The government is running us through the wringer in ways I would never have believed possible," Tony said. "You can answer any question they ask."

Through some type of government inquiry, my name had come up. I was mildly concerned, not because of any known wrongdoing, but because I just couldn't imagine what they might possibly want from me. The attorneys, I soon learned, wanted to know if there was anything untoward about our business dealings. Had I paid Tony money on the side? Did I consult for him, or him for me, outside of our company business? Did we have any written or oral side agreements?

To all of these questions, I could confidently answer, "No." Then came the Big Question: "Did you buy two Air Force Academy hockey tickets for Tony and his wife as a quid-pro-quo for business?" they asked with an air of conspiratorial interest.

"What?" I had no idea what they were talking about. "Well, we might have a problem." They referred me to Exhibit 37 displayed on the screen. "It shows here you made reference to these tickets in a business-related correspondence. The government has some concerns."

I was dumbfounded. With my now subpoenaed email displayed on the screen, I recalled that some years ago, Tony mentioned an upcoming trip to Colorado Springs, and that he'd love to take his wife to see an Academy hockey game. Tony was a friend, and another good friend of mine was the assistant coach, so I decided to help him out. A phone call later, there were two tickets at the will-call window. No funds were exchanged.

Years later, this innocuous incident became a government exhibit in building a case against someone who had done absolutely nothing wrong. I was sickened by the implication. They had their target in their crosshairs, and they were hunting for a crime! While you digest that scenario, consider that the price of each ticket was ten dollars. That's right, our US government that Tony and I had both served for decades was threatening serious criminal action over twenty bucks in gifted hockey tickets.

Three years of investigations later, neither the "hockey ticket incident" nor any other matter the feds investigated resulted in charges. Yet people's lives were seriously and negatively impacted.

Jeff's Story

When considering Jeff Martinovich's ordeal, Tony's outcome could have been much worse. What if they had pressed forward with an indictment and a trial? What if he refused to take a deal, went to trial, and lost?

If this happened to you, what would emerge from the ashes? Would you remain kind-hearted, cheerful, friendly, and loyal, planning your future with positive anticipation? What odds would you give that you'd come out of that scenario a better person than you went in?

In the case of Jeff Martinovich, we don't have to wonder. The story unfolds in the pages of this book. Jeff is a loving husband and father with a deepened sense of gratitude and humility, and he helps young business owners find their best path to success. His day is filled with value-enriching support for many people. How is that possible?

When I first heard about Jeff's very public misfortune, and being charged with serious crimes, I wasn't sure what to make of it. Had he done all he had been accused of doing? He and I met as incoming cadets to the US Air Force Academy in the summer of 1984. We were both recruited as intercollegiate athletes, Jeff for basketball and me for ice hockey. We quickly bonded as we realized most of our fellow cadets were more focused on the military aspect of the Academy experience. Despite adversity related to poor leadership and coaching on our respective teams, we both had the grit to persevere and eventually graduate. We were roommates for a time, and I considered him a close friend.

I quickly viewed my response to Jeff's predicament as a test of my own character and integrity. Loyalty is a personal value I cherish, yet I could not remain unflinchingly loyal to someone who had committed these crimes. The allegations certainly did not comport with my own experience with Jeff, so I decided to dig in and understand what had really happened.

At that time in my life, I believed much more strongly in the integrity of our justice system than I do today. I had spent twenty years in military service, and I wanted to believe real justice was the norm, injustice a rare exception. My belief in that system made me concerned that perhaps Jeff had somehow lost his way. In full disclosure, I was prepared to find evidence of his misdeeds when I went looking.

I dug in and researched everything I could find on the subject. I downloaded every case file and read every published article. In the end, I simply couldn't find an actual crime. If wealth and naiveté, sprinkled with a touch of ego and cockiness, were an actual crime, corner offices across the land would be empty. When I realized I was witnessing the most egregious miscarriage of justice I had ever seen, I became Jeff's staunch advocate. I remain so today.

The Right Thing

When adversity comes my way, am I ready to do the right thing? That's a question I've asked myself.

At the Air Force Academy, whenever we had to trudge up a steep hill on a march, or study day and night during finals, someone would quip "it builds character!" The idea that "adversity builds character" was a common viewpoint. In my experience, a better understanding is "Adversity *reveals* character."

The pressure of extreme adversity will tell you much more about a person's character than witnessing their behavior in good times. Jeff was subjected to the most intense adversity one could imagine, yet he emerged with a sense of dignity and honor. How did he begin a new chapter with grace and strength of character? It's all laid out in this book.

When Not If reminds us that adversity comes in many forms, we never see it coming, and it *always represents a test of our character.* Jeff has had a lot of time in prison—2,381 days and nights to be exact—to think about best practices when it comes to dealing with adversity. Consider his hard-earned prescriptions and be ready with them when you look up to find adversity breathing down your neck. By experiencing Jeff's journey through these pages, perhaps you will be more prepared for the inevitable crisis that will most certainly come your way. Be ready!

Jeff rejected numerous plea deals—the last one offered him three years, out in eighteen months—and he rejected each one because accepting a plea would require him to admit in front of his son that he intentionally broke the law when he knows he did no such thing. He knew that standing on principle might cost him a decade or more in prison. He knew that sometimes honor demands sacrifice.

Are you ready to make those choices?

I've achieved a level of success in my career. As I've moved along my own journey, I've been increasingly interested in the various ways people can get off track or worse. I study their adversity not to revel in their misery, but to viscerally feel their predicament, and then avoid it at all costs. If you combine a healthy skepticism of our institutions with a studied appreciation for what might trip you up, you might have potential elixir to avoid a similar fate. This book is filled with wisdom you should heed.

Jeff is arguably a better person today than before his adversity struck. Since he rebuilt his life, he is a better husband to his current wife Ashleigh and closer than ever to his son Cole. He has the same infectious energy he's always had, overlaid with a deeper sense of humility and gratitude. His sense of purpose has never been stronger, and he is devoted to his beautiful baby daughter, Carleigh. The friendships so critical to his survival remain strong, and Jeff works daily to repay the seemingly endless debt of support and loyalty his friends enthusiastically offered. As revealed in these pages, Jeff Martinovich knows who he is and what he's about, and I have no doubt he will come back stronger and healthier than ever.

Make no mistake . . . he didn't deserve to be sent to prison for his ambition, flashiness, or being less present than he could have been with his family. Who among us is not guilty of those offenses? Yet his transformation is an inspiration to us all, a great example of how we should arrange our lives right now, today.

Combine your powerful drive for success with thoughtful reflection on what is truly important . . . your values, your family, your close friends and colleagues. Love them, mentor them, and be available for them. Make sure the abundance you seek and will likely reap through focused effort is interwoven with gratitude and humility. If we all do that now, perhaps we can become better versions of ourselves *before* we face any major adversity. If we do, we will be better prepared for whatever might come our way.

BRIAN RADUENZ
Chief Executive Officer
AEVEX Aerospace
Solana Beach, California

PREPARE FOR ADVERSITY

IT SEEMED TO BE A PATTERN.

I was in disbelief. I sat on the floor of the majestic Clune Arena, where the US Air Force Academy Falcons basketball team competes, trying to make sense of the devastating announcement new head basketball coach Reggie Minton just delivered. Ten of the rising sophomores on the team had been summarily cut. Coach Minton was in. I was out. A new coaching staff was taking over and they had brought in their own recruits. The team was "going in another direction." My Division I college basketball career was over.

I struggled to understand how everything I had worked for could so arbitrarily be stripped from me. I had dedicated almost every waking moment of my youth to achieving a Division I basketball scholarship. And now an unforeseen authority figure had changed my life direction because he wanted to go "in another direction." How was this possible?

I loved basketball. At the same time, I was acutely aware the sport could be a means to an end. Given my family's economic reality, I knew a scholarship would be pretty much my only ticket to an elite college education, certainly one from such a prestigious institution as the Air Force Academy. I knew my limitations. Everyone was always

1

much taller than me, and maybe one or two were tougher than me, but I also knew my strengths. No one ever outworked me.

I spent my summers away at Indiana basketball camps purchased with the money I made mowing lawns. I ensured my grades were top of the class to increase my odds. I was so uptight I never even once drank beer with my high school friends. I couldn't bear the thought of one misstep destroying my singular focus on success.

I could understand if I had been cut because of merit or that someone else earned my spot because they outperformed me. But this was just one spring cleaning of dedicated scholar athletes. As I cleared out my locker, I suppressed both anger and tears of frustration. Paul Meyer, my power-forward classmate from San Antonio, Texas, raged, "This is bullshit! The coaching staff has their heads up their asses! The varsity are all losers who accept defeat game after game. And we're the ones clearing out our lockers?"

Paul's fury inspired me. The decision was final. We were out. But we could go out as winners. I led the sophomore team to challenge the varsity team in one last scrimmage. Five brave sophomores suited up and reappeared on the varsity court, challenging the starting team to an eleven-point blood match. Coach Minton cautiously agreed, no doubt hoping the varsity would confirm what losers we were. The whistle blew and we exploded with intensity. It was a physical contest beyond what our Western Athletic Conference referees would ever allow. My heart pounded out of my chest; my lungs still pained from the 7,000 ft. altitude of Pikes Peak. I gave this last quest for self-respect all the effort I had in me. After a hard-fought match, victory! The game was ours. The sophomores beat the starting varsity team 11-8.

This episode was my first major adult-life adversity challenge. It would hurt for a while and I would have to find another path, but I was proud of how I responded, how I stood up for myself. I could hear the Indiana coaches screaming, "It's not what happens to you that counts, but what you do about it!"

We rolled the ball back to Coach Minton and wished him luck. He would go on to a career of 161 wins and 311 losses. Back at Arnold Hall, named after the first general of the US Air Force, Henry H. "Hap" Arnold, chief of the US Army Air Forces during World War II, we celebrated with as much 3.2 beer as we could drink. Our fears and rejection had turned to hope and laughter.

Remarkably, I have remained close with my fellow cadets and teammates. Adversity builds special bonds.

> **The first lesson of adversity is that it comes unexpectedly and there's often nothing you can do to prevent it. All you can do is cultivate resilience, remember you are never alone, and pivot.**

So that's what we did. The Scrub Club, our self-applied moniker since we were unceremoniously scrubbed, turned to the top-ranked Air Force rugby program. For the next few years, I was fortunate to play for the first team and threw myself into the violent sport as a perfect release from the grueling constraints of the Academy. My senior year, we made it to the Collegiate Rugby National Championships in Monterey, California. I had started every match this season in the winger position and was eager to finally go out a winner, instead of a scrubber.

Then, Coach Barney pulled me aside one hour before the match and informed me that plans had changed, and the coaches had benched me in favor of our second-team winger. No good reason, no questions, just follow orders. After enduring one broken arm and two concussions for the team, I was once again out. My parents had used their savings to fly out to California for the championship game, and again I felt like I let them down.

> I learned the second lesson of adversity and made a vow to never again put myself in a position where my destiny depended on someone else.

Eventually, I decided I would start my own company, build the right A-Player culture, and as founder and CEO would finally be protected from the arbitrary whims of people with their own agendas. And for nearly two decades, the plan seemed to work beyond my wildest expectations. I believed I had been trained my entire life to build MICG Investment Management. The harder I worked and the more people I helped, the more successful I became. It made complete sense, and everything aligned.

In a blue-collar Virginia town, we, surprisingly, grew the firm to over $1 billion in assets serving 3,000 clients with a broad array of financial needs to include investment management, planning, lending, insurance, estate planning, investment banking, and more. We had one hundred associates serving clients in forty-six states and five countries, and I, again, believed there was no limit to our success.

I was wrong again. My new tagline "zero to a billion" almost overnight became "a billion to zero." This major black swan event crushed me, and everyone around me, more than all my previous failures combined.

> I learned the third lesson of adversity that it may take on many forms, which cannot be foreseen or even explained, but we must develop enhanced radar and wisdom to help us see around corners.

In short order, the company was closed, I was in a federal trial, and then I was sitting on a metal prison bunk for the next fourteen years of my life . . . until I wasn't. The pattern seemed to be continually repeating itself. I had received a master class in encountering and overcoming adversity, and while it's true we learn best from mistakes, these mistakes do not necessarily have to be our own.

The Book and Its Structure

This book is at once a travelogue into the world of adversity as experienced by one former CEO brought low by adversity and a leadership guide to recognizing and overcoming adversity in all its forms. This book operates on at least two levels to help you position yourself to be better prepared for black swan events of all varieties.

First, this book recounts my story as an object lesson in what happens to an individual unprepared to deal with overwhelming adversity. You may find my story instructive because whatever I did, initially, to deal with adversity, you should basically do the opposite. And I hope you find great inspiration in my actions to eventually overcome what everyone told me was impossible. I've had a lot of time to look backward and consider my mistakes. My hope is that by recounting my wrong-headed responses to my own adversity in some detail, I can help readers avoid some of the mistakes when they face their own black swan event.

Second, each of the eleven chapters distills three or four critical lessons that I eventually gained from my ordeal. Together, these lessons and takeaways unlock the tactical preparation and strategic responses that just might have prevented what happened to me. Certainly, had I heeded these practical guidelines, I would have been in a much better position to defend myself. These lessons are highlighted with borders to make them stand out from the text. I consider these lessons—won at such a high price—so important that they are assembled together at the end of the book. If you must read only one part of this book, I recommend you consider the collected lessons in the Summary of Lessons, Takeaways, and Best Practices.

In addition to the numerous stories and anecdotes in each of the chapters, I have four stories that work best as stand-alone interludes. I offer these stories so the reader can better understand the journey I was on and the emotional battering on individuals and their families adversity always takes.

For leaders and those who strive to excel in today's complex world of business, relationships, and connectedness, *it is not a matter of if, but when* will the black swan show up at *your* door. It normally occurs on a random Tuesday. My goal in this book is to allow you not only to learn from my myriad of mistakes but also to learn my hard-earned lessons and strategies which enabled me, step by step, to win a match that everyone said was impossible . . . and to receive miracles today which I cannot begin to explain.

CHAPTER 1

SURVIVE OR DIE

The world breaks everyone and afterward many are strong
at the broken places. But those that will not break it kills.
It kills the very good and the very gentle and the very
brave impartially. If you are none of these you can be sure
it will kill you too but there will be no special hurry.

—ERNEST HEMINGWAY, A FAREWELL TO ARMS

IT'S NOT EASY TO LOSE EVERYTHING that at one time seemed so important, so indispensable. My financial net worth was now zero. Less than zero if you consider I was in tremendous debt. All the tokens of privilege of a wealthy CEO were wiped away. My business, which I had built into a $1 billion success, was shuttered. The houses, the cars, the private jets, the golf clubs, the exotic vacations. All seized or evaporated.

Even my name became toxic. I was kicked off every board and committee. Every charity and philanthropy that had thought fit to honor me and my company by naming some program or high school stadium in gratitude for my donations quickly stripped off any recognition of my success.

And I was facing fourteen years of incarceration in federal prison.

Following the financial collapse of 2008, two neighbors, formerly successful financial advisors, took their lives. So many people were going through similar black swan events. Although we were not close, I quietly mourned their passing and prayed for their families. I remembered how this news had brought me to the brink of despair.

I had never before become so depressed and despondent that I considered taking my own life, yet now it was a very real consideration. My marriage fell apart. My ordeal killed my father. Basically I lost everything I had spent the first part of my career so zealously safeguarding.

I wrote two letters to Mission 22, the veterans charity focused on stopping the reported twenty-two suicides per day by our honorable warriors. I offered to help counsel struggling veterans and just be a pen pal and, possibly, save myself while saving someone else. No response.

Life-Altering Challenge

After my conviction for money laundering and fraud, I lost my name and became inmate 81091-083. Possibly the greatest challenge of prison is the loss of your name, identity, and everything that made you the person you were up to that moment.

FCI Fort Dix

The Federal Bureau of Prisons (BOP) saw fit to send me to the Federal Correctional Institution (FCI) Fort Dix, a dangerous US federal prison for male offenders in New Jersey—not one of the minimum-security camps normally housing white-collar inmates. It is the largest single federal prison in the United States based on the 4,000 inmates incarcerated there. I had to cope with being locked up in a brutal environment that was totally foreign to me.

Everything was loud—the metal doors slamming, the inmates fighting, the blaring announcements. The odors were overwhelming—the urinals, the trash, the men. The language was confusing— the prison gang vernacular, the dialects and accents, the shorthand and abbreviated communications. I, conceitedly, fought to maintain what I thought was standard English as a sign that I would eventually make it back out to my previous world.

Moves occurred on the hour, and this was the opportunity to change my environment from my bunk to work to the weight room. Moving meant I still had life, but the waiting to move would be excruciating. I couldn't understand why the doors never opened on time as I stood crammed against the metal and concrete with fifty other prisoners waiting for the guard to release us. I battled myself not to focus on the minutia of the life to which I'd been reduced. Why couldn't they serve the meals on time? Why couldn't the count be conducted on time? Why couldn't I maximize my day and accomplish as much as possible in each window I was given? As a business leader whose previous Outlook Calendar was separated into fifteen-minute increments, twelve hours per day, these miniscule battles were possibly the most challenging.

The prison supplies basically nothing more than a uniform. It was important to me to look as presentable as the circumstances allowed. I supposed it was my best shot at maintaining a form of dignity. Dignity in various shades of prison khaki is not easy, but possible. At least khaki was better than the orange jumpsuits, or paper jumpsuits, the institutions issued. I had my share of traveling in such outfits with hands and legs shackled as the BOP moved me from institution to institution.

I would purchase paper, pencils, typewriter ribbon, and toothpaste with the money my mother deposited in my prison account. I was humiliated that the woman I so proudly had rewarded with trips around the world was now having to send me money from her fixed income. This humiliation was only trumped by the infuriating rage I experienced when I periodically found my half-locker, holding my life possessions, broken into and my small cache of supplies raided. Theft was a constant. It was a part of prison life.

For the first few weeks of prison I was lost and groping for any semblance of normalcy. It was a dark time. I was disoriented, and hope was elusive. I called on all the reserves of resilience and bits of wisdom accumulated from sports, the military, and even the workshops I did with Tony Robbins and other leadership gurus. The power of those experiences would save me.

A Beginning and an End

I decided I was on a journey with a beginning and an end, hopefully. The end was too abstract to visualize. The beginning was very much in my face, so that's where I would start. Survival is a decision and I decided to survive.

In retrospect, I see so clearly I was meant to face this life-altering challenge. I realized there was no way the universe had prepared me with so many previous trials only to allow me to give up now. I constantly thought of my son, Cole, who was dealing with this radical life change himself in his own manner, the best he could. I stayed in contact with my mother as often as possible, as she was now all alone after the death of my father during my trial. I could not let them down, again. I could not leave them all alone, again.

And, finally, one morning while running the dirt track to get out just enough anger to make it through another day in the violent surroundings of FCI Fort Dix, I made a commitment to myself to never again think of this end to the story. I decided I had made it through the initial shock and despair of this existential encounter, and I committed to survival.

By the end of that self-imposed 10k morning run, I decided, "Hell, if I'm going to survive this horrific challenge, I might as well win." About the only thing they couldn't take from me was my competitive perspective on life. I remembered I had the freedom to choose my own point of view. That's the only thing any of us can reliably safeguard, and in the end it's what saved me.

A New Beginning

I didn't know exactly what "winning" looked like, so I started with a Life List.

In my cell at night, when the volume of shouting and the clanging of gates diminished to a low roar, I reviewed the lists I had made. I smiled ruefully at the long register of the amazing people I've known, loved, and helped, along with incredible people who had helped me throughout my life. I was ashamed that I had let so many of them down.

I decided to make another list. I had always been an OCD CEO constantly creating task lists for the day, the meeting, the project, and the next day, even putting items on the list after I completed them to get a little endorphin shot for checking another item off the record. This time, I made a list of all my incredible life experiences, categorized by People, Places, and Things.

As hard as it was to face my predicament, I was astonished at how focused and clear my mind could be. The most detailed recollections flowed from memory. I remembered the names of all my elementary schoolteachers, the names and positions of major league baseball players, and details of my high school teammates. I recalled my fifth-grade teacher, Mr. Haskins, who inspired me to "learn more than everyone else."

I listed my Air Force buddies who had stayed remarkably close to me through my ordeal. I listed the mentors who were so generous to me in the Young Presidents' Organization (YPO). From them I learned that success is not about how much you can take, but how much you give. I finally listed all the wonderful people who I had the honor to know and realized it was a miracle they showed me so much grace and love. I was determined to prove myself worthy of their support.

I wrote down memories of the fantastic places I had been fortunate enough to visit. Though I was at best a mediocre tourist, sadly indifferent to the sights and culture of foreign lands, the locals I met always fascinated me. I recalled my new friends in Vienna who stayed up all night with me at the blackjack table and then took us on the train to Budapest to see the buildings pockmarked with World War II bullet holes. I chuckled to myself as I recorded my days on safari at Kruger National Park in Africa. My party was shocked that rather than observing the lions and giraffes in the bush, I preferred to stay at the lodge all day with my new South African trail guides drinking Glenlivet and listening to their life stories.

I recorded the unique items I had been able to acquire and at one time seemed so important to me. I reminisced about my first car, a beloved 1975 Firebird I purchased for $500 earned by shoveling snow in my neighborhood. Though I owned many exotic cars since then, I missed that Firebird most of all. I kept these lists to myself as I came to understand from my cellmates that their own lists of possessions and opportunities, had they cared to go through the exercise, would be radically different.

I thought of the beach house that held many incredible family memories. The summer retreats with so many children, friends, and nourishing relationships felt like a distant other life.

This cathartic exercise seemed to peel back a thick layer of dread and pain and allowed me to realize once more how incredible my life had been. I quickly understood that, even if I never made it out of prison, I had *already* lived a life far beyond the bargain we make with heaven before coming down for the next challenge. I could breathe easier. I was almost able to look at my predicament from a third-party, objective view outside myself, and this helped me begin to strategize. I became so motivated that I instantly started on a new list of all the things I would accomplish and experience once I won this battle and got out of prison. A new *bucket list!*

I learned another simple tactic for overcoming adversity: Write down a list of all the people, places, and things you have been fortunate to experience in your incredible life. Then write a new bucket list of the amazing things you will accomplish once you figure out how to get outside the other end of this tunnel.

Don't dwell on how exactly you'll get there. That way frustration lies. Focus on the moment and incremental progress, and the journey will take care of itself. Think about taking a road trip at night. At any given point, your headlights illuminate only a few hundred feet of pavement. Everything else is obscured. But here's the point: you can make the whole trip that way.

A Little Stronger Every Day

My next lesson in overcoming adversity had to do with improving my personal situation in all the ways I could control. I didn't have control over what I wore. I didn't have control over where I slept or what or when I ate. Every door and gate was locked to me. Prison life limits everything. I had to find a way within these confines.

So I made a commitment to every day get a little stronger in the three dimensions I could control: physically, intellectually, and emotionally. In my former life as the CEO of a wealth management firm, I encouraged clients and employees to embrace the power of compound interest and continuous improvement. And now I put those tools to work to save my life.

So in the three areas—physical, intellectual, and emotional—I decided to apply continuous improvement at the rate of 1 percent per day.

PHYSICAL IMPROVEMENT

I knew physical strength and fitness would be required for my survival, but it's a misnomer that physical strength, by itself, will protect inmates from violence from fellow prisoners. Surviving prison, I soon learned, was 90 percent mental and 10 percent physical.

I was focused on improving my physical strength less for deterring violence against me from the outside and more to protect myself from the raging war inside my mind. I knew that daily workouts would provide the needed serotonin, dopamine, and endorphins necessary for positive forward progress and daily resilience to fight the good fight.

I hit the FCI Fort Dix weight room religiously. After the first couple of months, the gang members stopped asking if I was a "chomo" (child molester), the derogatory designation for sexual offenders. Chomos were not allowed in the weight room and took their lives into their own hands if they attempted to violate these rules. I ran the track every other evening, sometimes in prison work boots through the New Jersey snow, where I would find an hour of peace and tranquility, enabling me to visualize a positive future.

Just as Tony Robbins had taught me, I practiced smelling the beach, tasting the quality food, and feeling the touch of a beautiful woman holding my hand. Embarrassingly, I spent $3 per month earned at my prison 16-cents-per-hour job on a big bottle of cheap lotion. Each morning and evening my *cellie* made fun of me as I lathered up a thick covering of chemicals. I responded, "The haters are really going to be pissed when I come home looking younger than when I went in. It will be like it all never happened!" The extreme physical workouts allowed me to manifest victory, at least survival, and gave me the absolute strength to get up the next morning and do it all again.

For overcoming adversity, I understood the strategy of religiously committing to physical strength and fitness every single day. It was not an option, but mandatory. Whether part of our life already or a foreign practice, once the black swan shows up on a random Tuesday, we must dive into health and strength immediately in order to survive.

INTELLECTUAL IMPROVEMENT

Intellectually, I had been thrown into a world in which my prior education and training provided zero preparation. Federal criminal law might as well have been written in a foreign language for me. I knew I would have to devour every book obtainable and that trial-and-error would be my only path. I took a job as a law library clerk at FCI Fort Dix earning 16 cents per hour plus a rudimentary legal education. As I educated myself, I agreed to help every inmate who would accept my inexperienced but earnest assistance. I mastered law practice with a No. 2 pencil and manual typewriter.

One way I improved intellectually was by gradually becoming a decent jailhouse lawyer. Any time an inmate wants something to happen, it generally requires the preparation and filing of a motion. Fortunately, this can be done with, or without, the assistance of an attorney. Unfortunately, even when a nonlawyer inmate files this type of paperwork with the court without counsel, they must follow the same format and abide by the same rules that real lawyers are required to follow. If there's anything amiss, the motion is rejected.

Eventually through trial and error, I learned the rules and filed hundreds of *pro se* motions with the court. When my fellow prisoners protested that I was wasting my time, I exploded, saying, "Are you crazy? It's my only hope!" I had long given up hope that outside lawyers would or could help me.

Of course, the other inmates knew something my ignorance protected me from knowing. They were convinced there was, basically, a 0 percent chance of the court actually approving any motion filed by an inmate, or attorney for that matter. Their belief was continually confirmed by the nearly 100 percent failure rate. Not knowing how hopeless it was, I dove in and started filing everything possible.

On behalf of my fellow inmates and myself, I kept notes on the extremely low percentage of cases that were successfully reversed. I kept statistics on different elements of courtroom procedure. I journaled every tactic and strategy I thought might help them and myself. Just as in business when I attempted to be the smartest guy in the room, I wanted to become the smartest jailhouse lawyer in order to help as many people as possible, knowing that as I was helping other inmates, I was preparing to better represent myself.

I discovered most attorneys used templates, cut-and-pasted the same arguments from the other hundreds of cases they were handling contemporaneously. I learned how to use patterns that had been effective in other cases. I would periodically achieve a small victory. The Puerto Rican Latin Kings brought me Jose's letter from his attorney stating he did not qualify for the recent *drug-2 reduction* enacted by the Sentencing Commission. With a little research, I thought he had a chance, so we filed the motion and four months later we learned the court accepted our argument and reduced his sentence by three years. The Puerto Ricans always paid for services in *white lightening*, a moonshine derivative tasting worse than anything you can imagine.

I was never much of a fiction reader, so as part of my determination to improve intellectually at the rate of 1 percent per day, I made a decision to read a new book every few days. Luckily, the prison library had a collection of classic literature. Coming out of the engineering environment of the Air Force Academy, my knowledge of the classics was woeful. I knew this would likely be my only opportunity to remedy this failing. I read, and incredibly enjoyed, dozens of literary classics, and this escapism saved my sanity and helped me not become too hardened during this ordeal.

In a strange way, I am extremely grateful for this opportunity which I knew would have never happened unless I went through this challenge—a theme I would learn over and over before this adventure was complete.

> For overcoming adversity, early on I realized I must immerse myself in intellectual development and education in order to control my own destiny. I could not rely on attorneys, accountants, or industry experts to have the knowledge. I would have to find intellectual paths less traveled to be victorious.

EMOTIONAL DEVELOPMENT

Finally, emotionally and spiritually I realized I needed to find my North Star. I needed a purpose bigger than myself, and I needed to believe there was a grand design to this sometimes extremely painful life we lead on this planet. Without this *religion*, I knew I would never have the resilience or perseverance to survive long enough to possibly see restoration and resurrection. One major reason people give up is that they don't believe there might be a *life movie review* when passing on to our next adventure, or they don't believe there has to be some reason for our suffering or that we had even possibly chosen that suffering to make us a better being. I remembered how survival books always stated the great percentage of lost hikers gave up hope and perished within one mile of rescue.

Certainly through providence, my inmate compatriot, Ray, an Army lieutenant colonel who reenlisted to go to Iraq after 9-11, invited me to join him for a new Siddha Yoga Meditation program a New Jersey benefactor was offering in the prison chapel. After my initial, poor attempts at meditation, the organization would send me two substantial introspective reading lessons each month. These essays on the universe, life, meaning, and love calmed the rage that bubbled daily just below my Adam's apple and allowed me to function positively for one more day.

> When massive adversity occurs, such as the government knocks on our office door, or an unexpected event uproots and attempts to destroy our successful lives, we have to commit to something greater than ourselves. That's the essence of religion, whatever that may be for each of us. That something greater exists gives us hope that there can be a better life than what we have right now. Short fights, sprints, are possible through sheer will, but wars, marathons, require a belief in something deep, deep down in our souls.

On my classics list, I couldn't stop reading *The Count of Monte Cristo* by Alexandre Dumas, an 1846 novel about a man falsely imprisoned (you can see its appeal to me). The last sentence of this 1,200-page epic fascinated me. "Until the day when God will deign to reveal the future to man, all human wisdom is contained in these two words: 'Wait and hope.'" Ashleigh, my future miracle bride-to-be, in an act of solidarity would get a small tattoo on the inside of her right wrist with *hope* written in my handwriting.

CHAPTER 2

BLACK SWANS AND ADVERSITY

I've never forgotten for long at a time that living is struggle. I know that every good and excellent thing in the world stands moment by moment on the razor-edge of danger and must be fought for—whether it's a field, or a home, or a country.

—THORNTON WILDER

PRISON TIME IS DIFFERENT from everyday time.

A day in prison is a year and a year is a day. Here's what it's like in prison: days are so grueling and long and painful and frustrating that it seems like each day is an eternity. But it's also true that when you compartmentalize—a skill an extended prison sentence demands—years melt into each other. I look back on all those years and it's a struggle to believe I've been away from home for one year, five years, seven years. I wish I would have understood on day one of my adversity that the ordeal was going to last a multiple of ten times longer than I first thought, and it was going to be ten times more difficult to overcome than I ever first imagined. I wish someone explained to me it will not appear reasonable, or logical.

Only by changing my model of what constitutes arduous could I begin organizing my responses to adversity within the new set of rules and expectations. This shift in perspective gave me a fighting chance to not only survive but even thrive in conditions for which I was totally unprepared. Although the suffering of one day did seem to last a year from sunrise to sunset, when I look back, I cannot believe how much was endured, and how much was accomplished, in a year that seemed to fly by. "The bad news is time flies," observed motivational speaker Michael Altshuler. "The good news is you're the pilot." I was determined to be the pilot of whatever it was I would face.

Time on the outside was also flying by, I realized, with my large group of friends and associates moving on with their own lives. I, naively, wondered why they hadn't written. I constantly debated whether they thought I was a fraudulent pariah, or whether they just didn't care enough to check on me. I concluded it was likely a little bit of both, and people simply go on. While running the outside track, I would scream, "Who's paying their Bistro bar tab now?!"

First, I should have understood that not everyone around me is an ally and that even supposed allies may actually be adversaries. This thought is an anthesis to how I lived my life prior to the adversity that landed me in federal prison. When I was the CEO of MICG Investment Management, I believed everyone was mostly *good* and acted in good faith with good intentions.

For example, I believed all employees could be A-Players if I were only smart enough to recognize their unique gifts and reinforce them for success. I focused on helping people understand that their success and the organization's success were linked in a symbiotic win–win relationship. To the extent any of my employees underperformed I thought it reflected my own limitations as a leader.

Self-Interest

I also believed government regulators were organized to protect the clients of MICG Investment Management and to ensure fair dealing and to create a level playing field for the financial services industry. Instead, I should have internalized Adam Smith's teachings in *The Wealth of Nations*. In his 1776 book, Smith observed that *human beings everywhere work in their own self-interest*. How naïve and unsophisticated I was in dealing with the Securities and Exchange Commission (SEC) and the Financial Industry Regulatory Agency (FINRA), the main regulatory bodies ensuring the integrity of securities markets and the licensing and regulation of broker-dealers, respectively.

For almost two decades, the investment company I founded earned nearly perfect compliance and regulatory scores. Such an accomplishment was so rare the regional FINRA office termed MICG Investment Management "the golden child" for its pristine record of compliance. So when the senior leaders of the regional FINRA office requested our firm participate in a joint SEC-FINRA beta test to improve efficiencies for company audits, I agreed and offered up our resources to participate.

My decision here was a terrible one, flowing from a destructive combination of naiveté and ego. On the naiveté side, I really didn't realize that regulatory entities such as FINRA always have an adverse relationship with the entities they regulate. On the ego side, I was proud of how tightly MICG Investment Management was operating and I wanted to get credit for it. This appalling decision to cooperate, which unexpectedly coincided with the 2008 Financial Crisis in the markets and the outing of Bernie Madoff's $50 billion hedge fund Ponzi scheme, was the catalyst that set the investment firm I founded on its inevitable course to destruction.

FINRA's Thomas Hughes led a fishing expedition that seemed to operate with virtually unlimited resources against our operations, whose resources were more limited than they should have been. Our position was weaker than it had to be, and I fault myself for making us more vulnerable. I'll address these failures throughout the book. Meanwhile, the government was attacking us by death with a thousand cuts. They directed us to produce literally hundreds of thousands of email copies, then lost them, and demanded we produce them again. My IT bill was skyrocketing.

FINRA ordered our management team to visit their regional offices in Philadelphia. Clearly the attention on us was heating up. When we got there, the regulators proceeded to place upward of one hundred folders in front of each of us. Each folder contained printouts of conversations from the emails I had so naively agreed they could have to beta test an innocuous administrative system. Instead, the contents of those emails were being used against us. As he handed us a printout, and without context, FINRA regulator Tom Huber asked, "What do you think *was meant* by this email?"

Examining Emails

At first I was scared to death I would be presented with outrageous communications between our investment bankers, like the examples of financial malfeasance I read about each day in the *Wall Street Journal*. Or barring that, I'd have to explain emails appearing questionable only because they were stripped from context. In reality, nothing ever surfaced that worried me or even gave me pause. All the email threads seemed perfectly routine and innocuous. The other members of the MICG Investment Management team confirmed my sense that there was no there *there*.

That didn't stop Huber from asking about hundreds of emails. A lawyer by profession, Huber displayed a notable lack of sophistication about financial transactions. He asked such rudimentary questions about investments and hedge fund operations that I couldn't discern whether he was attempting to educate himself or bluff us as part of an organized ambush.

> But I had missed a cardinal rule of overcoming adversity: Never volunteer, offer information, or get involved willingly with the individuals and organizations charged to monitor, regulate, or penalize you. I facilitated them finding a case where there was no case to begin with. My foolish actions to volunteer, likely stemming from narcissistic desires to be important in our industry, served up our demise on a silver platter.

Seeing the Light

After nine months of this ongoing examination, a process I was told usually lasted an average of thirty to sixty days, I remember our long-term SEC contact phoning me to tell me the SEC had finished their review. Nevertheless, he told me, FINRA had the lead on this case since MICG Investment Management was a broker-dealer. The SEC contact also said two things he would later deny saying.

First, FINRA wouldn't sign off on the audit because, in the wake of the missed warnings about Bernie Madoff, every regulator was scared to miss something and put their own career at risk. Second, FINRA was focusing so much regulatory pressure on MICG Investment Management because it was not too small and not too large. In other words, we were big enough to matter but not big enough to put up a real fight. My contact told me to prepare for them to find *something*.

Again, I naively considered we would have to pay a fine and accept a mark on our otherwise unblemished record. It would be a bitter pill to swallow, but as this appeared to be the world we now lived in, I could live with it. I didn't understand the behemoth, entrenched administrative state arrayed against us.

FINRA claims to be a quasi-government agency that operates as a private organization not held to government accountability actions, while at the same time receiving government immunity when challenged by ordinary citizens. It is a giant agency that generates a substantial stream of fines and penalties in its enforcement actions. In 2021, FINRA collected $91 million in fines, according to FINRA, while the CEO Robert Cooke earned $3.12 million in salary along with a long list of executives all earning over $1 million themselves. As such, FINRA also operates as an entrenched technocratic state able to impose its own agenda. I was clearly losing to my first Goliath.

Some months later, unfortunately too late to help with our FINRA situation, a friend sent me *Three Felonies a Day: How the Feds Target the Innocent*, a 2011 book by Harvey A. Silverglate with a foreword by Alan Dershowitz. The book presents its own indictment and conclusion about the massive expansion of federal statutes.

The premise of *Three Felonies a Day* is that the average professional in this country wakes up in the morning, goes to work, comes home, eats dinner, and then goes to sleep, unaware that he or she has likely committed several federal crimes that day. The book argues that as the volume of federal criminal laws and regulations has exploded in number, they have become impossibly broad and vague. As a result, prosecutors can pin arguable federal crimes on any one professional for even the most seemingly innocuous behavior. The enforcement landscape becomes even more problematic for professionals as the statute books are augmented by the Code of Federal Regulations, which hands federal regulators an additional trove of vague and exceedingly complex and technical prohibitions to stick on their hapless targets. I wish I had read it sooner.

> This realization came too late for me to understand the fundamental adversity risk to every successful CEO and entrepreneur: If they enter your business, it is impossible for them to *not* uncover a long list of violations, and even felonies, with which they may choose to indict you.

Bedrock Shifting

I believed there was no chance anything like this could materialize in our organization. We were wildly successful and didn't need to cut corners. We had high ethical standards and trust in those we employed. I had never once had that *pit in my stomach* feeling that I could be breaking a law, or practicing activities that could even be perceived as unethical. I didn't understand the bedrock was shifting under me. I was a sitting duck for a black swan event.

The FINRA behemoth was well-staffed and well-experienced at executing their mission, just as happens with the virtually unlimited resources of the FBI, SEC, DEA, FDA, EPA, DHS, FCC, DOL, and hundreds of state and local agencies available to be called upon. The investigation continued for months.

On March 10, 2010, FINRA issued a news release. This tactic usually sufficed to destroy the beleaguered firms being targeted without a fight, rendering them incapable of defending their position. The next day, Peter Frost, writing for the Newport News *Daily Press*, reported, "The authority informed Martinovich and MICG on March 10 that it is preparing to bring six specific charges as a result of the investigation and offered the company a chance to submit an official response to defend itself. While FINRA has not yet filed formal charges, the notice it served to MICG signals that the regulator is at an advanced stage of its investigation and is preparing to levy charges." Dozens of other newspapers and websites picked up the news release.

The ensuing barrage of front-page articles made for a surreal existence.

- *MICG, Martinovich banned from securities industry*

- *FINRA Expels MICG Investment Management and Bars MICG's CEO for Fraud in Connection with MICG's Venture Strategies Hedge Fund*

- *Martinovich's riverfront home on the market for $2.6M*

- *MICG CEO Martinovich denies defrauding Newport News investor*

- *MICG's hedge fund investments in peril*

- *Head of Newport News investment firm, MICG, being investigated for fraud*

- *Local judges say, they can't hear MICG lawsuit*

- *MICG promised a silver lining in a cloud of mounting debt*

- *MICG ordered to limit trading*

- *EPV Solar, one of MICG Investment's star holdings, is bankrupt*

I struggled with "Do I hide?" or "Do I continue to lead my normal life as best possible?" Did one option admit guilt and the other show arrogance? I decided to hold my chin up, swallow the incredible guilt and anger, and show strength. My favorite advertisement has always been the US Marines commercial: *Toward the Sounds of Chaos*, which ends with "Which way would you run?"

I picked up my coffee at my usual Starbucks but left the line when a client spotted me and repeatedly shouted, "You should be ashamed!" I went to my regular Bistro Thursday happy hour, and two gentlemen got up and moved to the other end of the bar.

I did, however, make a showing to walk my son Cole out onto the Hampton Roads Academy football field to honor him for Senior Night, even though my picture had covered the top and bottom fold of the paper that morning. He was captain of the team that year, and I was not going to let my fear cause us to miss that special evening. My heart raced as we turned to face the packed stands of parents likely in shock that I would show my face before them.

Cole's own challenge to get through this time was my greatest pain, and the questions from his friends would both infuriate me and bring my greatest despair. But my role was to show him as much strength and grace as I could call upon. Otherwise, everything I had taught him in the previous eighteen years would mean nothing. I am incredibly proud of his strength.

I'm not sure what was the right path here, but I knew I couldn't win either way. Clients, shareholders, prosecutors, and judges repeatedly described my battle as exhibiting no guilt, no shame, and no regret. At this time, and for the ensuing decade, I decided to run toward chaos. I don't know if this was the right answer.

At times of extreme adversity, no one gives us a handbook on how to properly conduct ourselves. Every day and issue are new challenges we never expected to face, but if we can push fear to the side and draw upon our years of development and training, we can, hopefully, make more good choices than bad. But this is only for us to understand, and we cannot seek others to grasp our motives or approve of our decisions.

Existential Issue

As FINRA expected, the news that MICG Investment Management was under investigation became an immediate existential issue for the company. Clients already spooked by the turmoil in the markets in the wake of the Madoff scandal and the housing crash of 2008 began to run for the exits. Many of the advisors on the team also went to greener pastures.

Without an opportunity to utter a rebuttal, review an accusation, or even offer a resolution to any discrepancy, this public release had accomplished its mission. MICG Investment Management would have to close its doors.

It truly was genius, by design, as FINRA accomplished its goal to shut down a second-tier firm without ever going to court. Due process was not required. Proving or even explaining any allegation was not necessary. It was devastating. I raged with all the typical outbursts that evening, "How is this possible in the United States of America?!"

The reality is that I was completely outmatched. Our attorneys and accountants were outmatched. I now could see I was staring into the abyss. As the CEO of MICG Investment Management, once again I was defeated. As protector of our employees and clients, I had failed. As a father and husband, I had failed.

The $140,000 Motive

Nevertheless, I refused to accept what I believed were fabricated allegations. The regulators claimed MICG Investment Management had inflated the price of one private security, EPV Solar, in one of our three hedge funds. We priced shares of EPV Solar at $2.88 per share. The government argued that we criminally mispriced the shares, that $2.88 was too high, and the price should be lower. The government never specified what the proper price should have been.

And as for our alleged motive? The government claimed that I, as the CEO of MICG Investment Management, manipulated my management team, the independent valuation expert, and the licensed auditing firm to all place and approve a fraudulent price on this one stock in order for MICG Investment Management to receive $140,000 in unearned incentive fees.

At first, I couldn't believe the government was serious. Bernie Madoff reportedly stole about $65 billion and defrauded over 40,000 people from 125 countries, according to CNBC. Our holdings in EPV Solar represented less than 0.02 percent of our portfolio. Given that MICG earned more than $8 million in asset management fees the year the mispricing was said to occur, the allegation was little more than a rounding error. Ultimately, the government claimed I owed $2,471,399.22 in restitution through a series of mathematical gymnastics.

In those years, solar companies were the hot investment. Until they suddenly weren't. You may remember the Obama Administration's $2 billion loss on solar investments in the same period through the American Recovery and Reinvestment Act (ARRA). The most recognizable investment in those years was a company called Solyndra, a Fremont, CA-based manufacturer of thin film solar cells. Despite being heavily promoted as a leader in the sustainable energy sector for its unusual technology, it turned out that Solyndra was not able to compete with conventional solar panel manufacturers. About two years after the Obama administration cosigned $535 million loans to Solyndra, the company filed for bankruptcy on September 1, 2011.

Following the import of inexpensive solar panels into the United States from China—what the markets term *dumping*—over two hundred American solar companies collapsed and filed for bankruptcy. That included EPV Solar, which canceled its Initial Public Offering (IPO).

To me, the government's narrative was so fantastical that I couldn't accept it. To my core, I rejected the idea that we violated any rules much less that we did anything improper. I demanded we have our day in court, which in the securities industry meant an arbitration hearing in front of a board selected and compensated by the very organization alleging the violations. I knew the odds were against me, but I still believed in the system and I had to do something. I was grasping at straws.

There is a method of pricing assets such as stocks, options, and funds. It would take readers far afield from this narrative to get into the technical details; entire books have been written about the various methods of valuing assets. Here's how we handled the matter. Our practice at MICG Investment Management was to err on the conservative side and engage independent valuation experts to help us price new assets. Although hiring outside experts is not a requirement, that's exactly what we did when we needed to assign a rational price for

EPV Solar. We engaged an independent solar industry expert named J. Peter Lynch (not to be confused with Peter Lynch, the legendary investor and founder of The Magellan Fund).

Testifying to Valuation

At one point in the trial, J. Peter Lynch was called to testify. Lynch was sworn in and took the stand as an expert government witness. Under examination, Lynch described the calculations he used to assign a value to EPV Solar. This went to the heart of the matter as the government's predicate for the charges against me were based on the prosecution's argument that the valuation was unfairly priced above what it should have been.

Lynch testified the value adopted for shares of EPV Solar was a rational one based on objective criteria. This portion of the trial transcript can be found in its entirety in the Appendix. Here's an excerpt of the highlights of Lynch's direct testimony, starting on page 445 of the official transcript.

> QUESTION: When you fixed it on the last amount of $2.88, you felt that also was a reasonable figure based upon the value of the company?
>
> LYNCH: Correct.
>
> QUESTION: And in the attachment you say, "consequently it is my conclusion that the share value of $2.88 and the overall company valuation of approximately $500 million arrived at earlier in this memo is conservative," correct?
>
> LYNCH: Yes.

QUESTION: And the share value of $2.88 is highlighted, correct?

LYNCH: Correct.

QUESTION: And by signing this you are representing the contents of that valuation under your signature, correct?

LYNCH: Correct.

Following the testimony of J. Peter Lynch, the financial auditor. Michael Umscheid, of Harbinger PLC, was sworn in. He testified that in his expert opinion, the calculations of the valuation expert were accurate and the valuation of $2.88 per share could be defended as reasonable:

UMSCHEID: (S)o my audit was focused on the cash transactions in and out and the valuations of the companies that the hedge fund held . . . because of the bond raise (Jefferies & Co. $77 million raise for EPV Solar) there was an intrinsic value to the stock of $2.88 per share, based on the bond raise . . . Yes, I—I approved—I gave my opinion that the asset value that they put at $2.88 was reasonable, yes. [Tr. p. 2453, 2532, 2542]

Pressure Mounts

Friday, May 7, 2010, just after the 4:00 p.m. markets close I received a phone call from FINRA regulators. They abruptly told me, "The exam has *switched gears*. FINRA has re-audited the last five years of financials for MICG. We have reclassified shareholder contributions as debt." Based on the structure of our holding companies, this major balance sheet change required us to deposit millions of dollars on

Monday morning before the 9:30 a.m. opening. Otherwise, the firm was not permitted to operate.

The Uniform Net Capital Rule is very complex. Basically, the SEC requires broker-dealers to have enough cash in the bank to meet their financial obligations to clients and other creditors. We always complied with the requirement to have sufficient liquid assets to pay for all our liabilities and to still retain a cushion of required liquid assets (i.e., the "net capital" requirement) to ensure payment of all obligations owed to customers if there was a delay in liquidating the assets. But the news release FINRA had posted and its last-minute reinterpretation of our capital position put us in an existential bind, and they knew it.

Under normal circumstances, we could have negotiated a short-term bank loan to satisfy the capital demand. But after the allegations, with MICG Investment Management on the front page of the financial section of every newspaper in the region, no bank in the land would provide a twenty-four-hour credit line to satisfy the conditions FINRA imposed.

Once these allegations were released to the press, what I thought to be close relationships and grateful connections evaporated overnight. Paul Trible, Jr., the president of Christopher Newport University, asked me to resign from the board of the Luter School of Business and discontinue granting scholarships. Hampton Roads Academy took down the MICG Park signage on the new baseball stadium but didn't return my check. I was asked to resign from multiple charity boards. The board of The Children's Village of Hampton Roads, a charity I founded, actually voted to disband.

The government and public narratives were so powerful that clients and shareholders unwittingly worked tirelessly against their own best interests. The frenzy created lawsuits, testimonies, and direct actions from the very people who would be hurt most by the collapse of the entity and people stewarding their investments. This was my first exposure to the environment in which I would later learn to succeed only by creating a new description, "Up is down, and wrong may be right, but it is what it is."

Why Kill the Golden Goose?

I never understood why they had to kill the golden goose. If the regulators truly believed I had masterminded a fraudulent scam, then why didn't they just fine, censure, prosecute, and bar me, the founder and CEO, from the securities industry? Instead, they, overnight, shut down a company that supported the lives and families of so many people—employees, clients, vendors, shareholders, charities, and community partners.

I had believed the mission of regulators was to support the best interests of the clients and customers. It did not appear to be a concern, even when we repeatedly proposed MICG could change any pricing in any manner regulators felt more accurate. Tom Huber and FINRA associates, as well as later Assistant US Attorneys (AUSAs) Brian Samuels and Katie Dougherty, would never tell us what, in their estimation, the adjusted price should have been.

Our attorneys and accountants were able to negotiate a 7:30 a.m. Monday phone call with the regulators in order to, hopefully, find a resolution to this latest condition. I didn't believe that FINRA really wanted to destroy MICG Investment Management, frighten thousands of clients, and throw dozens of innocent employees out of work. The lawyers reminded FINRA that the multiple business lines of MICG Investment Management had been routinely audited and FINRA itself had signed off on *those very financials* for the past five years. The lawyers respectfully asked FINRA to grant more time for us to demonstrate compliance.

My management team and auditors worked all weekend to prepare for the Monday morning meeting. At exactly 7:30 a.m. that Monday, as FINRA had agreed, we placed a call to Tom Huber, hoping in good faith to resolve the matter. After multiple rings without anyone picking up, we started to worry. We repeated the call at 8:00 a.m. Then at 8:15 a.m. and 8:30 a.m. No one at FINRA would pick up the phone. We gradually understood that we were being ghosted. Eventually a FINRA receptionist came on the line and claimed that Huber and the regional FINRA regulators were in a meeting and could not be disturbed. We were bureaucratically outplayed. And now we were out of time and options. Without an approved net capital computation, it would be illegal for us to trade securities for our clients or for their own accounts.

Out of Options

At 9:25 a.m., I was forced to make a firm-wide announcement that MICG could not open its doors for business. We were out of business. Finished. Just like that, it was over.

The immediate fallout was predictable and devastating. Clients, employees, shareholders, friends, vendors, charities, and everyone ran for the doors. Building managers locked me out of my own offices. I moved into the Marriott Hotel and then an apartment as my marriage crumbled. Almost immediately, Sheriff's deputies began serving lawsuits at my front door. There were so many, I started to know the process servers by name. My inner circle of loyal teammates stacked boxes of client files in my bedroom, and it seemed that every person in the country had my cell phone number and was calling every hour of the day and night.

In one last effort to honor our clients, my remaining team processed transfers in my kitchen all hours of the day and night to facilitate account changes to other brokerage firms. Emotions ran high. Associates and friends trying to help would suddenly begin crying. I felt as if I were holding my breath swimming to an ocean surface I could never reach.

Following two weeks of utter chaos, FINRA relayed a final settlement demand to my lawyers, Benjamin Biard and Todd Lynch. The message required me as founder and CEO of MICG Investment Management (The Respondent) to sign an Offer of Settlement. If I resisted, my lawyers were told that FINRA would revoke the trading licenses of the brokers on my team. I was willing to forfeit my own license and accepted being barred from ever working again in the securities industry. But I wasn't willing to let my brokers go down with the ship.

I carefully read the language in the Offer of Settlement, and here is an excerpt I carefully read many times:

> *Respondents submit this offer to resolve this proceeding and do not admit or deny the allegations of the Complaint. Respondents also submit this offer upon the condition that FINRA shall not institute or entertain, at any time, any further proceeding as to Respondents based on the allegations of the Complaint, and upon further condition that it will not be used in this proceeding, in any other proceeding, or otherwise.* [See the Appendix]

I took some comfort from two of the stipulations that FINRA obligated itself to in the Offer of Settlement. First, that in resolving the matter, the Respondents do not admit or deny the allegations.

That was important to me because I honestly thought it would be dishonest of me to admit to conduct I, or anyone else on the team, felt we did not do. Two, I accepted at face value FINRA's agreement that it would not proceed with any further action against me.

The Unsettled Settlement

For a week, the Offer of Settlement sat on my kitchen table as I consumed a worrying number of Goose martinis and had loud conversations with my attorneys. My options were dwindling. More outrageous from my point of view: the FINRA settlement was structured as an *offer from me*. FINRA wanted me to represent to the world that I had requested the terms of the settlement and, further, to affirm that I had not been coerced or extorted in any manner.

The position of my lawyers was consistent: settle. "Why are you still fighting this?" my attorney Benjamin Biard said. "They won! You've already spent $400,000 on legal fees and it will be another $200,000 to defend this, and what are you defending? Everything is gone!"

On the sixth day, I signed the Offer of Settlement. I have regretted the decision every day since.

> I would later learn another key lesson for overcoming adversity: Fight your battle early. If you appease the black swan instead of confronting it and standing up for what you believe is right, it can rapidly expand into an overwhelming and unmanageable, even existential, challenge. Be Churchill, not Chamberlain.

Above All, Communicate

I made a huge mistake by not attempting to release our own narrative. As all business leaders know, the attorneys' first instructions are to never say a word, to not speak to investigators, to not respond to reporters, and to not promulgate your own press releases.

I now believe this to be a terribly wrong strategy. Of course, never agree to speak to the police or FBI without an attorney present. But in terms of operating in today's online, interconnected world, it's critical for any beleaguered firm to have a narrative that can be offered as an alternative to the version of events represented by critics or regulators. Otherwise, the narrative of the adversaries, unrefuted, becomes reality so much that it becomes almost impossible for anyone to consider an alternative is even possible.

"You need a story to displace a story . . . ." Nassim Taleb writes in *Black Swan*, "When you develop your opinions on the basis of weak evidence, you will have difficulty interpreting subsequent information that contradicts these opinions, even if this new information is obviously more accurate."

Another critical rule for overcoming adversity is we must communicate our own narrative. Perception is reality, and vacuums will be filled by your opponents if you do not act quickly and decisively to control the information. If you don't control your narrative, your adversaries will. Remember the wisdom of Gordon Gekko in Wall Street: "The most valuable commodity I know of is information."

I failed by not speaking our truth. My first step should have been to engage a crisis communications firm to help us shape and publicize a more correct version of the story. The vacuum of information I tolerated caused all our stakeholders to rely on whatever the newspapers would print. And since we weren't talking, the media had little else to go on but the government's self-serving news releases.

It was my responsibility to speak up for my company, my employees, and myself, but I blew it. Fear can be crippling, and I did not have the courage to stand up to Goliath at this point. Although now, there is no way to know for sure, it's possible that had we mounted an aggressive media campaign standing up against what we perceived to be an ill-advised prosecution, we might have secured some allies and the regulators may have backed off in part or in whole.

Not communicating forcefully was one more critical error that sealed my fate, and created so much economic pain for so many people undeserving of distress.

CHAPTER 3

LEAD YOURSELF BEFORE LEADING OTHERS

*Adversity has ever been considered as the state in which
a man most easily becomes acquainted with himself.*

—SAMUEL JOHNSON

THERE WAS A TIME WHEN HONOR was so sacred that people literally staked their lives on it. For the Founding Fathers, honor was so important that it's literally the final word in the Declaration of Independence: "And for the support of this declaration . . . we mutually pledge to each other our lives, our fortunes, and our sacred honor." Each of the Founding Fathers accepted that by signing the document, they were signing their own death warrants in the event the British prevailed. History shows that the leaders most revered take their honor seriously.

Allegiance to some system of honor has been a part of my life as long as I remember. It was modeled by my parents. By the time I became a cadet entering the US Air Force Academy, I promised myself I would live up to the fundamental requirements of the honor code, and like every cadet, I took the Honor Code Oath as part of my participation in the Acceptance Day Parade, when I was formally recognized as fourth-class cadet.

The Honor Code Oath simply states that "We will not lie, steal, or cheat, nor tolerate among us anyone who does. Furthermore, I resolve to do my duty and to live honorably, so help me God."

Honor

When I was interviewing candidates who wanted to join MICG Investment Management, I would sometimes ask them what they meant by honor. There were a lot of furrowed brows and bewildered looks. If I was lucky to get an answer out of a candidate, they might say that honor is about respect and standards and dignity. And those things are part of it. But there's more.

To me, real honor is the foundational building block of leadership. It is not the fake political honor professed by *bureaucracies* or *cogs in the machine*. It is the true trust and respect my close circle of friends describe as "the character you want with you in that foxhole." Honor means adhering to the same standards the leader holds others to and is the bond between an individual and a community expressed as a code of conduct that tries to balance what is right for the individual and just for society.

Leadership is an honor that should not be taken lightly. When it comes to leadership, honor is expressed as stewardship. The universal temptation of leadership is for leaders to use their position to leverage personal gain. The selfish perception—"that leadership should have its advantages"—is, actually, dishonorable. Leadership does have its advantages, but in a way opposite to the intentions of entitled leaders.

Leadership is about stewardship—an opportunity to give of yourself so that you can make a difference for those you serve.

"A man who has nothing which he is willing to fight for, nothing which he cares more about than he does about his personal safety, is a miserable creature who has no chance of being free, unless made and kept so by the exertions of better men than himself." I had to memorize dozens of quotations about honor, ethics, and leadership, but I was stunned when I read this one, attributed to the British philosopher John Stuart Mill (1806–1873) in *Contrails*, the handbook for US Air Force cadets. The handbook contains aircraft nomenclature, famous quotes, poems, and songs that cadets must memorize during their time at the Academy. I yelled out these quotes and aircraft designations while being trained by overbearing upper class students or being pushed under the barbed wire by obstacle course cadre.

Mill's definition that conflates honor and leadership always struck me more powerfully than all the rest of the duty and honor quotes and lessons I was forced to cram into memory. Little did I know how critical these values would become during my later most difficult challenges.

Making a Bargain

During my nightly prayers growing up and throughout my leadership of MICG Investment Management, I silently asked God to let me lead a *life of significance*. I wanted a consequential life that left the world better off for having me in it, and I wanted it to matter that I was here! I thought my life and career would be a series of incremental victories and successes. Little did I understand that leading an amazing life, the ones of great epics and documentaries, always involved failure and tragedy before rising from the ashes. Inside FCI Fort Dix, my fellow inmate, Colonel Ray, an American patriot who had rejoined the Army after 9/11 but now faced a similar battle to myself inside prison walls, taught me the proper storyline slope of a good novel, and he stressed, "No one is interested in a continuing upward slope of success! That's boring! There must be a huge dip! There must be tragedy!"

I would bet that if you took a poll of inmates who had an opinion about the Bible, a majority would say the character they most identified with was Job in the Book of Job. I have come to view the predicament that brought me so low akin to the kind of adversity faced by Job. My faith in a benevolent world guided by a benevolent spirit was tested almost to the breaking point.

Most people think of Job as the rich man in the Bible who lost it all and gained it back. As I read the story, I resonated to the fact that Job, despite crippling adversity, consistently displayed character in the sense that he acts, thinks, and feels in a way that is inspiring. At night after a particularly difficult day, I would frequently flip to this story.

Only much later did I realize that one reason I admired Job so much was because he himself must have been a leader. The way the Bible described his wealth and holdings, Job must have employed hundreds of workers to manage his lands and livestock. The Bible doesn't say much about his management skills but instead focuses on his character as a leader and moral rectitude. I took this as the first leadership lesson of Job.

Leaders understand that they will be tested by adversity. Success rarely comes easily, and when it does, there is every risk it will eventually disappear. Leaders understand that success must be earned and that it cannot arrive without patience and struggle. Nothing is more fragile than success that appears effortless.

Massive, Positive Forward Progress

I knew I would have to hold on to hope. Focusing on my shame, regret, guilt, and self-pity would accomplish nothing. Worse, it would hold me back. I saw much evidence of this among my fellow inmates. Those who wallowed in their predicament usually gave up and instead of doing the time in a constructive way, they let time do them. And take my word for it, time in prison is a punishing superintendent. It's true that the prison administration is set up to strip inmates of any power or agency they might possess. I understood that only massive, positive forward progress daily, with a trajectory I did not, necessarily, yet understand, would remedy the pain I had caused by my horrific series of failures. It was like swimming against the tide. Massive riptides could drown me at any time.

When I was the CEO, my goal was to hire and lead only the most qualified professionals. I understood that if I were going to be able to hire and lead A-Players, they would only follow someone they felt to be equal to or stronger than themselves.

I had a number of quotations ready for any occasion. "Leadership by example is the only leadership which still works in this world," was one I shared with my colleagues whenever I had an opportunity to address various teams. As the CEO, I usually got to the office before anyone else. I wanted them to see my car in the parking lot as they drove up. I made coffee for everyone in the office in part to demonstrate that the CEO was not above kitchen duties. I wanted to model a style of leadership they would accept as stewardship in that my main goal was to walk the walk and do everything possible to be a positive example.

Corporate Culture

As I had years behind bars to think about it, perhaps some aspects of the corporate culture I was determined to cultivate were over the top. For example, at the firm's annual retreats, me and my president Steve would wake up the newcomers at 3:00 a.m. and challenge them to push-up contests. This after the entire team had a rollicking night with stupendous consumption of food and drink. I was determined to demonstrate the leaders were stronger and more capable than the rising wolves who we were convinced would soon challenge for the right to lead the pack. I couldn't silence the mantra *the strength of the pack is the wolf and the strength of the wolf is the pack.*

Others may say my behavior was too competitive. Looking back on it, I'd have to agree. When having the privilege to recruit successful financial advisors from UBS, Morgan Stanley, and Merrill Lynch, I ensured, outside of my CEO role, that my personal book of business always surpassed everyone else in order to gain the respect of over-achievers we desired to recruit. Every time a teammate whined that the work–family balance prevented them from hitting their target, I pulled out my list of every sports team I was currently coaching for my son and the vacations I had recently taken with my family.

Now, in a completely different environment and experiential journey, I knew I had to lead myself, and in turn, I could possibly lead so many others to better outcomes. I quickly learned that, at a minimum, just helping other *colleagues* have hope gave me incredible power and hope to help myself. Courage is contagious. But, I also remembered, talk is cheap, and everyone can be motivated for a sprint. I had the marathon to conquer. My courage was severely challenged in the Spring of 2012.

The Arrest

At 7:00 a.m. on Friday, October 12, 2012, a team of FBI, Treasury, and IRS agents broke into my apartment with automatic weapons drawn. Just like in the movies, the plainclothes agents shouted "FBI." The agents ransacked the apartment and made Rebecca dress at gunpoint as she cried in humiliation. They handcuffed me with my hands behind my back and dragged me down the long hallway of our building while other tenants opened their doors to watch the spectacle.

Outside was a row of dark SUVs with their lights flashing for effect. The agents pushed me into the back of the middle car, my hands still behind my back, strapped me in, and sped off in a parade of sirens and lights.

The Perp Walk

At the courthouse, the photographers and camera operators were thick as I was exposed to the news media in the uniquely American ritual known as the "perp walk." This is the part of the booking process in which the accused is ceremoniously led into a police station or courthouse in such a way as to promote the media's ability to capture the event.

Still lost in my self-absorbed world, I thought of the terrible images to appear in the next day's newspapers. In my vanity I lamented my appearance supplemented by 20 pounds around my middle from the martini depression diet that had recently sustained me. I knew the newspapers would make hay with those photos, and they would follow me around for the rest of my life. No matter how much I possibly redeemed myself, they would never lose their power. The photos of my perp walk will be published as part of my obituary.

Now I was inside the jail. I was marched by a row of cages, all filled with angry looking men hurling insults at me. Above the general roar of abuse, I could hear one inmate marveling, "Who's the white guy in the Gucci's and True Religions?!"

I gathered I was being marched to a holding cell. I passed "A-Block" as the men leapt into the glass walls, pounding, and hammering like a scene out of a demented zoo. I prayed to myself, "Lord, please don't let me be assigned to A-Block!"

Meanwhile, my friends and corporate attorneys scrambled to find an attorney practiced in federal criminal defense work. These were a class of professionals I certainly did not have on speed dial, never imagining I would ever have an urgent need for such contacts. I cooled my nerves for a few days and then it was Sunday. I had a visitor. His name was James Broccoletti, a partner with Zoby, Broccoletti, PLC of Norfolk, VA.

From behind glass, I regarded my new criminal defense attorney. Broccoletti was well recommended. He is an active member of various bars and associations, including the American Bar Association, the Federal Bar Association, the Norfolk & Portsmouth Bar Association, and the Virginia Beach Bar Association. He serves on the US Sentencing Commission Practitioners Advisory Group to represent the Fourth Circuit.

He started asking me questions. Immediately after, I recorded our conversation with a tiny pencil on the back of the Western Tidewater Regional Jail (WTRJ) Inmate Manual. My training told me to document every conversation and instruction, something which would serve me well for nearly the next decade.

His first question was, "So, what did you do when the feds sent you the Target Letter?"

"What letter?"

He looked confused. "Well, what did you say when they brought you in for the meeting to discuss the allegations?"

"What meeting?"

"You mean they just broke into your home with a warrant and dragged you down here with no warning?" Broccoletti asked.

"What warrant?!"

Exceptional Case

At that point, Broccoletti began to understand how exceptional, or more correctly, problematic, my case was. He went to work getting me—someone accused of nonviolent offenses with no criminal record and deep ties to the community—out of jail. It should have taken hours. It actually took five days.

Five days after I was arrested and booked, I was released on my own recognizance. I would later understand this *bureaucratic snafu* while watching *60 Minutes* in the prison television room. It was an attempt to soften me up to accept the plea deal the US attorney would inevitably offer me. It was surreal to watch an episode of the CBS news program *60 Minutes* in the jail common room that dealt with the Fed's deliberate ploy to scare white-collar defendants into taking pleas by making their initial jail experiences as frightening and degrading as possible. Their goal was to get a quick conviction and move on to the next target. This would be my first exposure to the orchestration of a system I never knew existed, much less contemplated a need to understand.

> When adversity shows up on our doorstep, we have to instantly realize we don't know what we don't know. My biggest mistakes, at the most critical moments, came from my overconfidence in believing I was smart enough to navigate these treacherous waters. I should have accepted that this game had a completely different set of rules. I should have, also, allowed my planning and strategy to be open to terrible outcomes and possibilities I dreaded. In a sense, my overconfidence and previous success blinded me to the fact there was an extremely high probability that the battle I was fighting was already lost.

As I listened to my attorneys, my overconfidence continued to rule my strategy. Broccoletti and his team encouraged that overconfidence. It was a warning sign I ignored. When we sat down for our first meeting after my release, Broccoletti told me, "We've reviewed the government's discovery, and we can't find one piece of evidence that shows you did anything wrong. If anyone even did anything wrong it would have to be the guys in New York!" He was referring to the consultants we hired to evaluate the asset in question.

I leapt out of my chair and yelled, "That's what I've been telling everyone from the beginning!"

"Samuels [Brian Samuels, the lead AUSA prosecuting the case] offered seven years, and I already told him 'no way'," Broccoletti said.

Rejecting the First Plea Deal

It wasn't hard for me to reject the offer to plead guilty in exchange for a sentence of seven years or eighty-four months in prison. I learned that federal sentences are often doled out in as months of incarceration as determined by the Federal Sentencing Guidelines. These are rules that set out a standardized policy for sentencing people who are convicted of felonies in federal courts. The goal was to create more consistency in sentencing across the United States. The two factors that most determine the length of a sentence are the nature of the crimes and the criminal record of the defendant.

Over the next few months, the government gave us increasingly sweeter offers. The US attorney's office wrote my lawyer that in exchange for pleading guilty I could serve five years or sixty months. I met with the attorneys again, and they repeated their claims the government had zero evidence of my wrongdoing. "The only thing that worries me is if they parade twenty-five grandmothers up to the stand who say you stole their money," James Broccoletti warned. I rejected the US attorney's offer of five years. Broccoletti's prescient caution would later be validated at trial when the prosecution put a long parade of elderly clients on the stand to testify against me.

As the date for the start of my trial grew nearer, my 24/7 anxiety increased. Broccoletti called me in for a final strategy meeting. This was on a Friday. "I spoke to [Assistant U.S. Attorney] Samuels and the government is now offering three years or 36 months," he said. "But he won't put the offer in writing this time since you rejected the last two. There's a drug and alcohol rehabilitation program we could get you into which knocks off a year, and with good time you could be out in eighteen months." Broccoletti told me I had to have an answer by Monday.

Sentencing Guidelines

And then he really got my attention by pulling his copy of the US Federal Sentencing Guidelines off his shelf and flipping to the table regarding the crimes I was accused of. He looked up at me and made sure I was paying full attention. "If we lose at trial, you could be looking at ten-to-twelve years," Broccoletti told me.

Although we had covered this ground many times before, I again asked him to take a deep dive with me into the evidence against me. The discovery process revealed what evidence the prosecution was prepared to use against me. I confirmed one last time that his team had found no evidence connecting me with any wrongdoing. I confirmed he felt confident the jury would see there was no wild conspiracy or effort to manipulate any pricing.

Then I had to make the toughest decision of my life. I spent the weekend talking to my father, talking with my son, and double checking with my prior management team that I had not missed an obscure violation.

I spent time with my son, Cole, and sought his advice. I had tried my very best to instill in him a sense of honor and the value of honesty. Should I settle or should I go to trial? Cole was noncommittal. It had to be my choice. He reminded me that he was going off to college and assured me he would "be fine" with whatever course I chose. He wanted me to make the call unburdened by what the impact of my decisions might have on him.

I was reluctant to further burden my father with this dilemma. I remembered an episode from his early years. My father's father left the family when my father was born. Although my grandfather continued to live in the same city as my father, he never once had further contact with his son. I could never understand that level of indifference and it frankly made me both furious and broken-hearted on behalf of my father.

When my grandfather finally died, I was stunned that my father decided to go to the funeral in Johnstown, Pennsylvania. I remember protesting his decision. How could he honor the man who abandoned him? My father responded that he was paying respect *and doing the right thing.* I reminded my father that he had never once met any of those people and that if it were me, I'd tell them all to go to hell.

His words from that day informed my decision about whether to take the plea deal or go to trial. In response to my bitterness, the simplicity was powerful. He affirmed, "Sometimes in life you do the right thing simply because it's the right thing to do." Now, was it my time to do the right thing during what appeared to be the greatest challenge of my life?

Reconciling Theories

For my part, I struggled with the fact that in my heart I simply could not reconcile the government's theory of the case with my own conduct, or the actions of my team. I scrutinized my conduct on every level and while I made my share of mistakes, to my mind, nothing I did rose to the level of criminality, or even approached unethical. My consultants and legal team agreed with that position.

I knew that accepting the plea deal was certainly the expedient thing to do. Doing so would provide me and my family with some real benefits. First, it would confer a degree of certainty in a process that was otherwise quite unpredictable. Second, a plea deal would eliminate the need for the painful and costly experience of a trial in federal court.

Modeling Integrity

My decision had lots of facets, but perhaps my main consideration was how it would look to my son and my corporate teammates who had built something special to stand up in court and dishonestly admit to shameful conduct that occurred only in the theory of the prosecution. I had always counseled everyone else to always stand up and do the right thing, especially when the stakes were at their highest.

I now came to the crux of my decision. If now, during my life's most severe challenge, I didn't stand up for what I believed, if I accepted a plea under such circumstances, would everything I had worked so hard to instill in my family, my teammates, and myself be worthless?

I realized the hardest decisions facing a leader aren't between right and wrong, but between integrity and expediency, knowing that both decision points have unpredictable costs. It's easy for leaders to do a cost–benefit analysis and to take the path that seems least costly in the moment, to do what's less painful, to ease uneasiness with an expedient decision just to avoid tackling the pain the right path imposes. "The truth of the matter is that you always know the right thing to do," said General Norman Schwarzkopf, Jr. "The hard part is doing it."

> Overcoming extreme adversity often demands we make one or multiple pivotal decisions. Yet, if throughout our life we take on challenges others shy away from, and we build as much character and positive success in our memory bank as possible, we may have enough courage to make that truly existential decision we always hoped we could handle. These prior training grounds give us the confidence and energy to be the leader we always hoped we could be.

The Most Consequential Decision

So now the time was up. I had to make the most consequential decision of my life. I pause here to ask the reader to consider what you would do when faced with a similar decision. Suppose you sincerely believe nothing you did was wrong. Suppose you are offered a deal to plead guilty with the certainty you will lose your freedom for thirty-six months and be branded a convicted felon for the rest of your life. Or you can reject the plea offer and take your chances with a jury. Your bet may pay off. The jury may come back with a verdict of not guilty and the ordeal is over. Or the jury will convict and then you will certainly face a sentence four or five times longer than the plea deal guaranteed.

Here's what I decided.

I rejected the third plea offer and chose to go to trial against the unlimited resources of the US government, knowing full well the opposing team boasted of a 98.5 percent conviction rate. Naivety could have motivated the decision. It could have been false bravado where I manipulated myself into thinking I was a valiant hero in my own epic. It could have also been a blind fear of having to admit guilt and failure to everyone I had so vigorously worked to convince I was a good person. Many people say I'm an idiot, and I cannot present a good argument to the contrary.

People constantly ask me, if I had the chance to make the same decision again, after knowing the horrific costs of the choice I made, would I make the same decision?

Yes, I would.

CHAPTER 4

YOU ARE ALONE

Adversity is like a strong wind . . . it holds us back from places
we might otherwise go. It also tears away from us all but the
things that cannot be torn, so that afterward we see ourselves
as we really are, and not merely as we might like to be.

—ARTHUR GOLDEN

WHEN IS IT EVER JUSTIFIABLE in a system of laws and rules to completely obliterate your adversary?

In *Black Swan*, Nassim Taleb writes, "You can afford to be compassionate, lax, and courteous if, once in a while, when it is least expected of you, but completely justified, you sue someone, or savage an enemy, just to show that you can walk the walk."

This truism was modified and turned against me by AUSA Brian Samuels, who in court and in numerous subsequent appeals repeatedly labeled my efforts to defend myself as "scorched earth strategy."[1] In what version of a judicial system based on the presumption of innocence is it reasonable to villainize the defendant's choice to defend himself? By this reckoning, my attempts to prove the truth were characterized as an egregious act against the state and the people. Never did I feel so disadvantaged and alone.

> Although family, friends, and institutional placeholders may attempt to support those who are in the crosshairs of federal prosecutors, defendants must accept that they are ultimately alone. They must take personal responsibility for every action and subsequent outcome in order to survive and make it out *the other side.*

It was ridiculous of me to think that my legal team supported by a small battalion of accountants could rescue me. They were so many gnats the government mostly ignored. The facts bear an inescapable conclusion. My fate was predetermined on an institutional basis and the outcome was inevitable. Unfortunately, I was not educated enough to see that. I could blame my attorneys and accountants for failing to educate me, but the responsibility was mine to see the reality of the situation.

Sadly, I failed to see something even more insidious. I failed to grasp that I was but one defendant in an endless line of defendants. Long after I was locked up and forgotten, my lawyers would have to interact with the US attorneys on other cases. They would have to work with the same clerks and bailiffs who kept the court running. And they would have to appear before the same judge who sentenced me.

It was delusional of me to think James Broccoletti, my attorney well known for knowing his way around the US District Court for the Eastern District of Virginia, would risk alienating the professionals he would have to work with again on countless future cases.

He represented me professionally and by the book, but I learned that there were limits to how zealously he would stand against the prosecution determined to destroy me. I should have better understood the position of defense attorneys in the system and how they generally dare not push the system too hard lest they jeopardize their own interests.

My ego was so large I couldn't understand the influence and control a long-term US District Court Judge like the Honorable Robert G. Doumar must hold over courtroom proceedings and the eventual outcome from a jury.

Death in the Family

As we prepared the final push for trial, Doctor Mattern, of the Virginia Oncology Associates, and a long-term family friend, called. "Jeff, I know this is not the best of times for you, but I have more bad news. Your father has stage 4 lung cancer and it won't be long." Don Martinovich had retired from thirty-five years of civilian service in the Foreign Technology Division (FTD) of the Air Force spending his days protecting the country he loved from the Soviet Union and communism. His nights were spent in the service of capitalism and building a better life for himself and his family.

My father had taught himself the ins and outs of capitalism with particular emphasis on real estate accompanied by a religious serving of Lord Calvert Canadian Whiskey. Growing up across from the gates of Bethlehem Steel, without a father in his life, he personified the American dream, and I always knew whatever hard work and values I had inside me were a response to the way he handled his own hardships.

Following his retirement, I had talked him into working *special projects* for me, moving him and Mom down to Virginia, and for nearly fifteen years allowing him to spend every day with his new grandson, whom he adored. Now, his last moments would be consumed with my great failure and disappointment. I was crushed he would not be around to see me *fix* this debacle. He had taken my downfall, our downfall, extremely hard, and I am convinced the incredible stress accelerated his cancer and shortened his time with our family. We had always overcome our challenges, together, but, this time, his last view would be complete destruction.

His cancer accelerated and hospice took over very soon after. I fought with lawyers all day, and each night I tried to bring him relief with tales of our past triumphs and stories of how I was going to win this battle against Goliath. He would repeat, "Never let the bastards get you down."

James Broccoletti called me to let me know the prosecutors, AUSAs Brian Samuels and Katy Dougherty, wanted to postpone the trial start date due to my father's imminent passing. At first I was touched by what seemed an ounce of compassion from our foes, but James quickly explained they do not want my father to die in the middle of trial and the defense to receive any sympathy from the jury. I would just have to attend a quick hearing with the Honorable Judge Robert G. Doumar to implement this delay.

Here Comes the Judge

This was my first exposure to Judge Doumar, a legendary federal judge in Norfolk, Virginia, and I was also, of course, hoping to make a good first impression. Apparently, somebody beat me to it. This would be the first time I was blindsided by the actions of the courtroom, but certainly not the last. After the lawyers presented the quick background for the hearing, eighty-three-year-old Judge Doumar, who initially looked like any other gentle grandfather I may have known, began aggressively interrogating me from the bench about items I had no idea how to answer.

His Order released to the press stated,

> "[T]he Court found Defendant's testimony to be equivocal and evasive. Defendant is allegedly well-versed in the provision of financial services. Though claiming to handle finances for his parents since his father fell ill, Defendant was unable to answer even basic questions concerning their capacity to afford third-party care. Even questions concerning his personal finances drew vague responses. For instance, prior to the hearing the Court learned from pre-trial services that Defendant's recent monthly expenses included: (l) $2,100 per month for a 3-bedroom condo in downtown Norfolk; (2) $475 per month for payment on a recent model year Audi A6; (3) $995 for dining out; and (4) $200 per month in utilities...When questioned about that rather large budget for dining out, however, Defendant claimed to not know what the Court was talking about. Moreover, Defendant provided inconsistent testimony in some respects."

> "In light of Defendant's equivocal and evasive testimony during the November 28, 2012, hearing, the Court declines to credit his claim that he intends to spend significant time caring for his terminally ill father in the coming months... Therefore, the Court DENIES Defendant's Motion to Continue Trial insofar as it is based on Defendant's

alleged need to care for his terminally ill father" [Doc. 30. 11/29/2012].

I will have more to say about Judge Doumar in Chapter 7.

Again, I didn't ask them, they asked me. But each ruling, just as I learned with the FINRA settlement, always would reverse the proceedings into a request, or offer, from me.

The prosecution later proposed a postponement based on workload to achieve their objective, but this theater had, seemingly, accomplished the purpose of positioning the case, and myself, as the wealthy, equivocal, inconsistent, evasive, and, of course, guilty defendant for the public and all parties. What suddenly terrified me at this moment was the wakeup call that not only the prosecution was positioning this strategy but also the Honorable Robert Doumar. Maybe I should have reconsidered those three plea offers.

But, instead, my competitive and immature anger caused me to dig in my heels further and vow to win this battle, with Don looking over. I began to realize my defense attorney, James Broccoletti, was not in control of any part of this process, and that the prosecution, pretrial administrators, and apparently the court itself were all aligned with the same objective. Outside of my remaining friends who were helpless in this federal world with its own rules, and my faithful mother showing up each day to support me just as we see in countless court hearings for minorities annually, I was alone to fight this fight and pull off a victory that everyone told me was impossible.

I lived in a fantasy world, and my naiveté and passive reliance nearly sealed my fate. I should have known better. I had built a successful business on the understanding that humans will always work in what they regard as their self-interest, but for some reason, in this foreign battle my insecurities had me believe that all these *experts* would seek the truth and a logical resolution. My self-confidence blinded me at this most critical point in my life when I should have been applying long-term leadership and organizational behavior experience.

PAWN SHOPS AND BLACKJACK TABLES

THE NUCLEAR FALLOUT of the closure of MICG swarmed around me. Beleaguered as I was, I took stock of my situation. Money was quickly flowing out the door. I don't care how much money you have. When you spend $55,000 in monthly bills going out, and your income drops to zero overnight, that loud sucking sound you hear is your money market account being depleted. Guilt stopped me from cutting up the ex's Platinum American Express, and her justifiable anger at me was expressed in a purchasing extravagance worthy of any American Idol winner.

Barred as I was from the profession I knew best, I threw my energy into consulting engagements designed to grow sales and revenues for the companies of three friends. And though my friends were more than satisfied with the results my work generated, I was not successful in winning business from people that didn't already know me. I call it *The Google Factor.* Just typing "Martinovich" into a search bar instantly created page after page of *make sure you run from this guy as fast as possible!*

Meanwhile I had a family to support. That I managed to do, just barely. But my income simply could not match the outflow to attorneys, forensic accountants, expert witnesses, storage facilities, and other costs that my defense team required.

I took some comfort from being on the long tail end of commission checks flowing predictably from Fidelity, Oppenheimer, John Hancock, and a long list of previous investments partners. I wondered how long these would last. As expected, the checks slowed to a trickle until one day the mailbox was empty.

I racked my brain to find a short-term solution for some income. I felt if I could survive just long enough I could fix this debacle, rebuild, restore, and write a successful final chapter to this nightmare story. I would not allow myself to think how unlikely this successful final chapter was.

Then as I walked back from the mailbox one day, disappointed that there were no window envelopes containing a much-needed commission check, I saw a mailer from the Bellagio Las Vegas Resort. In better days, I organized annual golf trips to Vegas for my close circle of Air Force friends. As a result, the mailer reminded me, I had earned a substantial Bellagio VIP account. These credits covered the cost of rooms, food, and even entertainment. Moreover, the mailer reminded me, I had a $20,000 credit line awaiting one last chance to allow me to survive just a little longer. I was what they called a whale. Little did they know I now felt more like a minnow. All I had to do was arrange the flight and the rest of the expenses were complementary. Desperation leads to desperate thinking. A plan started forming in my mind. All I needed was one lucky break.

I sat in my small kitchen and considered whether gambling really was the answer to my misfortune. I asked God if my plan was more insane than everything else I had tried. The money was gone. The credit cards maxed out. The stack of bills was getting ever higher. New lawsuits arrived daily. I didn't have any better idea. All I had to do was to get to Vegas and try my luck.

There was only one problem. I didn't have money for the airfare. Then I looked at my wrist and the one remaining artifact I had from my fat cat days. It was my last asset, a Cartier Roadster watch. So I googled "Pawn Shops" and made my way to the closest, Nathan's Lynnhaven Pawn Shop. I introduced myself and tried not to look desperate. Moments later I was out the door, my left wrist bare, but with $4,000 in my pocket. My first purchase was a one-way flight to Las Vegas.

I knew this plan represented a one-time last shot the universe was offering me. I booked three days to allow me to implement a cautious, by-the-book blackjack strategy. I promised myself I wouldn't drink any Glenlivet until I finished playing for the day. This may have been the most difficult part for me since I had set brand-new records for day drinking since my ordeal began.

At the Bellagio Las Vegas Resort, I pulled down $20,000 off my credit line, and with my blackjack rules card tucked in my coat pocket, I sat down at a table and made my first wager.

Day one was up a little, day two was down a little, and my brilliant idea seemed to be little more than holding off the inevitable. The third day was no better. At least I was even for my efforts.

Then, the third, and last, evening was upon me. My luck turned and I started to win. I increased my bets as the forward progress continued. My heart pounded with fear *the fates* would turn on me and take it all away. Still, the stack of colored chips in front of me kept growing. Some people noticed and a small crowd joined in the fun. The pit bosses kept their eyes on the table and awaited my likely, eventual downfall. But the stacks in front of me kept growing. I was practicing my math skills to track the cards and counts. I prayed I would know when *enough is enough* and I could get up and walk away.

An hour later, I estimated that the stacks of colored chips in front of me represented $60,000. For once in my life, I had the discipline to say "Stop!" Enough is enough. I wished my new friends at the table future success, tipped the dealer well, and *colored up* my chips. I had the presence to *not* pay off my credit line for the moment, as I knew I needed every cent of my replenished war chest for what lay ahead of me.

I walked down the long Bellagio hall to the Petrossian piano bar by the entrance. I added to the glass tip jar on the piano and requested some Frank Sinatra and a martini. I sat at my table overlooking the flow of gamblers, few of whom would be as lucky as me on this day. I raised my eyes and said, "Okay, for some reason, You just won't let this end. There has to be a reason why You won't let me die." It was my first experience with the power of the *grand design*.

Over and over for the next decade, through the pain, I would experience incredible breaks, rewards, and good fortune which, inexplicably, enabled me to keep going one more day or to find motivation to believe, eventually, everything was going to be okay. But, for this moment, I simply enjoyed an amazing martini and, knowing I had a few more months of runway for my defense, watched the eclectic world flow by.

CHAPTER 5

GIVE MORE THAN YOU TAKE

The Purpose of life is to be defeated by greater and greater things.

—RAINER MARIA RILKE

MONEY AND I HAVE ALWAYS had a sympathetic relationship.

By that I mean there was never a mystery to me about making money.

The most reliable path to making money is working harder than anyone else, but understanding the concept of helping other people get what they want can be equally as important. It's rarely about being smarter or taking shortcuts. While many times it helps to be born into a family with means, I have found just as many other times it's a hindrance to developing the work ethic and mutual cooperation necessary to develop wealth.

The family I grew up in was middle-class America. My father worked hard and we had a roof over our heads. But there was little slack in the family budget for nonessentials. I quickly learned that if I wanted to buy something for myself, I would have to earn the money to buy it. In earlier chapters I described the jobs—the lawn mowing and snow shoveling businesses—I took on to earn whatever money I needed. I was fortunate to receive on-the-job training and begin to understand the rewards of hard work and exceeding customer expectations.

I applied that work ethic to my first job in financial services with results that, fortunately, exceeded everyone's expectations. My first role was as a rookie financial advisor with Wheat First Securities in Newport News, Virginia. Newport News is a blue-collar shipyard town, and I recognized many of the people I first represented. They reminded me of my own parents: hard-working, no-nonsense people who earned everything they owned and maybe could afford $100 per month to invest in a retirement account.

Operating at Disadvantage

At the same time, I looked around at my fellow career-entry advisors and quickly saw I was operating at a disadvantage. Many of my fellow newcomers came from families with money, and many were experienced businesspeople. As a result, I knew that if I was going to succeed, I was going to have to outwork them many times over to be number one.

The good news in the advisory business is that there's a direct relationship between helping the most people and realizing great success yourself.

Plus I liked helping people. Everything about the good part of the finance industry seemed to make sense to me, and I devoured my new opportunity.

But since I had to open five to ten times more accounts than my experienced classmates to achieve the same results, I set out to make friends with as many people as possible, and to take on any breathing human as a new client, regardless of how limited their short-term prospects appeared to be. My father had faith in me that I would excel and I transferred that attitude to every one of my prospects. I treated every person—in elevators, coffee shops, bank lobbies, the car wash—as a potential client even if it was likely they had never met a financial advisor. When I wasn't talking to strangers, I was dialing for dollars. I learned how to be outgoing, introduce myself, speak up, and figure out what help people needed and offer it to them.

As a result, while my competitors were opening up the occasional million-dollar portfolio, I focused on becoming king of the $100-per-month-into-mutual-fund-accounts-club. It turns out that getting to first base every time I came to bat was often a superior strategy to striking out repeatedly going for the home run. I didn't know it at the time, but I was pursuing the counterintuitive premise the 2011 movie *Moneyball* validated. The secret to building a financial services practice, just as in baseball, is to get on a base a lot. It doesn't matter if it's a walk or a hit. To get wins, you first have to get on base.

Since I had to open up so many more accounts than my fellow advisors, I had to reach out to dozens of new contacts every day. By outworking my colleagues and simply making as many new friends as humanly possible, I was building a book of business and relationships which would ultimately make me the number one advisor. Because I could not yet afford membership in the country club, I spent day and night cold calling. I spent Saturdays making presentations in the back room of The Golden Corral. And I spent countless evenings providing seminars for the local Rotary and Kiwanis Clubs. Other times I presented financial planning sessions at the local library, many nights to a crowd of just one or two people looking for help, but I learned those who showed up were the perfect people for me to pursue. I never wasted time focusing on the people who weren't there. I knew I'd run into them eventually.

I was learning one of the key fundamentals for overcoming challenges and adversity.

> Help as many people as possible, and the universe will, in turn, reward you with results and victories far beyond what you, and everyone else, believed was possible. It is a mathematical truism. It was the law of attraction before I even knew the meaning of the phrase.

Daily Opportunities

I opened new accounts for our firm at a rate they had not seen before, and although my average account size was modest, each day a new opportunity from the universe would present itself as a reward for having so many new clients, many of whom regarded me as a friend. The successes of my clients became my own.

Joann received a promotion at NASA where she was an engineer and phoned me to increase her monthly withdrawal to her retirement account. Susan received a sizable inheritance, quadrupling the balance in her account. Frank retired from the Newport News Shipyard and rolled over his hefty pension account to my stewardship. And Thomas finally accepted an offer to buy his HVAC company and, now a rich man, deposited much of the proceeds into his investment account where I could make him (and myself) even wealthier.

This large client base, coupled with the continued growth from referrals and introductions, resulted in tremendous growth for our business, especially as the asset numbers expanded with the fortunes of my clients. Over nearly two decades, our business grew an average of 36 percent year-to-year, a strong record of continuous growth. This is how I went from the rookie who knew nobody to one of the most influential people in our community and industry. My Rolodex had the names of the most generous and community-minded people in the area. If there was to be a philanthropic event or great party, I was often the first one called to share my Rolodex. Just as Einstein believed the power of compound interest was the eighth wonder of the world, making so many new friends compounded into incredible opportunities for me, my family, and our business—and some epic parties!

Rebuild My Database

And then adversity hit. I lost my Rolodex and the goodwill of the contacts in the database. After much success and wealth, I was reduced to zero. Everything I had worked so hard to build was forfeited. Money and influence? I had none. And even my right to freedom was taken away.

There really was only one thing not denied me. I seized the only certainty left to me. After all I had lost, I could start over. The adversity only intensified my desire to work hard and rebuild. There was no room in my worldview for cynicism, self-absorption, or self-pity. Indulging in any of these life-is-unfair, woe-is-me attitudes would guarantee defeat.

I forced myself to reach out in a strange new world, again. I took a job in the FCI Fort Dix prison law library, where, if there were any keys for my escape, that's where I would find them. I volunteered to help other inmates building resumes and practice interview techniques. I created a twenty-five-lesson course titled "Building Special

Companies," which I taught at night to an unexpectedly eager crowd of budding entrepreneurs. I tutored inmates to pass the General Educational Diploma (GED) exam, a surprisingly difficult preparation process.

I recognized that in prison, much like in the outside world, sports and recreation are often paths to trusting relationships. When I was CEO, I saw more deals consummated on the golf links than in the boardroom. So in prison, I played centerfield for the unit softball team, with shoes two sizes too small, to ingratiate myself with the significant Latino population in the 4,000-inmate prison. I was the point guard for the unit basketball team to build relationships with the even more significant Black population. I have a prized photograph that shows me as the only Caucasian member on the All-Star team. There was not a lot I could control, but my attitude and capacity for finding new friends were about the only things still under my control.

I reminded myself daily to help as many people as possible, in the knowledge that this approach was my only chance to help myself. When faced with extreme adversity, we must accept that our previous database, our previous life, will likely be erased, but a new database is always available for construction.

From Zilch to Effective Assistance

My knowledge of federal criminal law was zero, but I had a neverending flow of clientele eager for any assistance possible. Usually these conversations started with a desperation to vent about the horrific legal representation they experienced. I could relate but kept the focus on their cases. They recounted the churn of court-appointed attorneys, the lost paperwork, the missed deadlines, accepting they were interchangeable components of a legal assembly line, of no more individual interest to their counsel than the staples keeping their paperwork from scattering in the wind.

I had set the goal of improving myself by 1 percent per day in three dimensions, and the first dimension was intellectual. Pretty soon after starting to help inmates with their legal questions, I began to see patterns in the paperwork. Despite the many differences in the charges and legal circumstances of each inmate, the paperwork looked suspiciously similar.

I was reminded of what I learned in my MBA classes and business manufacturing and accounting courses. The best businesses run on consistency. But what's good for businesses may not be ideal for individuals dealing with unique legal challenges. Nevertheless, the legal paperwork I was looking at displayed the same maddening characteristics.

First, the indictments alleged the same crimes. Then the plea agreements applied the same enhancements that lengthened the inmate's sentence above what the Federal Sentencing Guidelines prescribed. Moreover, there was always similar language that offered the inmate a reduction in his sentence on the condition they testified against another defendant, or the threats of indicting a family member. The language denying every one of the court-appointed defense attorney's motions was little more than boilerplate.

Revolving Assembly Line

It really was a revolving assembly line, only now the business auto-mation software was controlling human lives, not widgets. Identical paragraphs were cut and pasted by the prosecution, and identical paragraphs were cut and pasted in response by the appointed defense attorney. It struck me what a waste of a law school education it would be to deal with defendants by endlessly duplicating templates over and over. And how dehumanizing for the attorneys as well as the defendants.

I began to understand it was such a numbers and volume game, and this was why criminal attorneys had to take on so many clients. This system couldn't possibly deliver adequate response times or service to clients. Most shocking to me was the negligible difference in results achieved by wealthy white-collar defendants and the indigent inmates who asked me to write their motions.

I met a number of fellow inmates who spent literally millions of dollars on white-shoe law firms for representation, firms like Williams and Connolly, Kirkland and Ellis, and Jones Day. The inmates' des-peration and the panic of their families induced them to part with millions of dollars in the hopes these celebrated law firms could provide meaningful relief. In almost all cases, they did not. My cell mate, Richard, a famous cardiologist whom they alleged, ironically, helped *too many* patients, sheepishly admitted to me he had paid over $5 million for his trial defense and, after conviction, millions more for appeal after appeal.

Out of intense fear and hopelessness, defendants bleed their assets down to zero and later regret how these clever attorneys destroyed what security they had left for their families. I began to see the tremendous ecosystem which lived off the high-volume rotation of humans through the federal criminal justice system.

Regulatory Capture

In economic terms, what I was seeing was a version of regulatory capture. Regulatory capture happens when a system that is supposed to regulate a process or activity becomes dominated by the interests they are charged with regulating. The result is a system charged with upholding the legitimacy of the judiciary profession instead acting in ways that benefit incumbent firms in the profession it is supposed to be regulating. This dynamic happens because these industries maintain a keen and ongoing interest in influencing government regulators, whereas ordinary citizens spend only limited resources to advocate for their own personal rights.

At the time of my indictment, I was the YPO chairman for the State of Virginia. I had learned the collective strength and influence of our global network of CEOs could accomplish pretty much anything. All it would take was a well-placed telephone call from the right advocate. I said to my attorney, James Broccoletti, "This is absurd! Who do I call?" His response, "For this, there's no one to call."

When faced with extreme adversity, even ones that may take our liberty, we have to understand the wealth we built over all these years may have little impact on our likelihood of success, or even survival. Our money cannot free us. Even the most powerful, connected CEO must pivot and return to relying on their own abilities and the goodwill developed by helping others.

But I was learning. I began to learn the game, and soon I was copying the same paragraphs, defenses, filings, and procedures used by the court-appointed attorneys. I made a practice to research Latin legal terms, such as *void ab initio* (literally void from the beginning, an action that is not enforceable because it never had any legal effect). I inserted these Latinisms in each new motion just to try and add a little excitement to the process.

Periodically, the court clerk writing the judge's response would repeat my new term in the denial, either to make his own life a little more interesting, or more likely to mock me for attempting to have success against the system. At the District Court level, as well as the Appeals Court level, newly minted law school graduates read the great majority of motions, reflexively dismiss the merit of a great majority of the motions, and compose the response for the judge's signature.

Despite the fact that ninety-nine times out of a hundred, the motions I filed on behalf of my fellow inmates and myself were summarily denied, or never received a response, I filed literally thousands of motions, petitions, and letters over the years I was confined. What other option did I have to help these prisoners, and maybe help myself? It was a numbers game akin to the financial advisory business, what we earlier termed the theory of "n," referencing it's all just mathematical equations. My cold calling "n" had been "89," which meant I had to dial 89 numbers from the phone book in order to get one prospective client to agree to a meeting. I noted the irony of how closely this number matched my dismal success ratio presenting motions to the court.

Small Victories

Then, every once in a great while, I would experience a small victory, such as when a US Supreme Court case would set a new precedent with which we could file a novel petition to apply these interpretations to an inmate's case and get some relief. A few cases redefined what constituted certain acts adding mandatory minimum sentences.

Consider the case of an inmate I'll call Sammy. A *bunkie* in my twelve-man room at FCI Ft. Dix, I got to know Sammy well. His was a typical story of drug-addict parents abandoning him, raised by his grandmother in Troy, Ohio, a boxing background, and his six-foot, eight-inch frame made him an incredible basketball player on our team. I knew he could probably have had a big-time Division I college career if he had simply experienced a middle-class upbringing like my own. He was serving a twenty-year sentence for brandishing a firearm during an altercation at a bar. Every one of my bunkies had firearms on their list of charges. It was simply a way of life. It would be incomprehensible for them to think about *not* carrying a firearm. The dichotomy of life experiences always struck me in dealing with these cases. Knowing my own competitive nature and love of leadership, I always thought of how, given different circumstances, I would have very likely been the top gang leader and top drug salesperson for my city. Luckily for me, I had so many more options.

Gary, a fellow prison law clerk much smarter than me, took the lead on Sammy's case. He spent innumerable hours researching and writing while I did my best to add value and draft a compelling narrative. It worked. After many months we received notice that Sammy would be heading to a minimum-security camp and then be released ten years early. We were in shock and delighted by the radical impact our efforts had on Sammy's life.

That evening in my room of twelve metal bunks, Sammy got into an argument with Alex the *store guy*. The *store guy* is normally an inmate with access to funds who buys extra commissary—drinks, packs of tuna fish, oatmeal, peanut butter—and then sells it at a markup. Just like on the outside, people are willing to pay extra for convenience. We were allowed to go to the commissary but once a week, so most of us were willing to pay a little more for items without waiting. But not everyone.

Sammy didn't like the high markup Alex was currently charging, and Alex, a man of small stature from Guatemala, made the mistake of commenting on the virtue of Sammy's mother. Respect is very important in prison and must be maintained. Disrespect in prison can lead to extremely violent situations.

So it was in this moment. Sammy hit Alex over and over, and Alex dove into Sammy's knees and held on for dear life, a tactic the smaller inmates used when faced with sure destruction. Sammy didn't enjoy hitting Alex on top of his head, so he began to violently choke him. I don't know what compelled me, but I ran across the room and, literally, jumped on Sammy's brawny back, grabbed him around the neck, and screamed, "Stop! You're going to a camp! You're going home! Don't destroy it all now over a packet of tuna fish!"

Sammy released Alex, turned to me with a stare looking deep off into something, and said "Thanks," and walked back to his bunk. For Sammy, it was over as quickly as it started. Not so for me. That evening, I sat up most of the night in my top bunk vibrating with the adrenaline the episode released. Eventually, I relaxed and contemplated what we had done. Was it a victory Sammy was being released, or was it a terrible mistake that would befall some other store owner in Troy, Ohio? There was no way to know. I remembered a line from Henry James's *The Middle Years*. "We work in the dark—we do what we can—we give what we have. Our doubt is our passion, and our passion is our task. The rest is … madness."

I hated the system. I hated the universe. I hated my life.

CHAPTER 6

MODEL INTEGRITY

*In any moment of decision, the best thing you can
do is the right thing, the next best thing is the wrong
thing, and the worst thing you can do is nothing.*

—THEODORE ROOSEVELT

NOTHING BRINGS OUT THE BEST and worst in people like a federal criminal trial.

Everyone's self-interests are on full display for the world to see—except they're not. Unlike proceedings in state criminal justice systems, federal courtrooms do not permit cameras or audio recordings. I could not understand how we allowed that restriction in the United States of America.

Therefore, the world's interpretation of the events must be filtered through the lens of the government's accusations, the writings of the federal judge, and the interests of the newspapers. My friends, kindly self-labeled as *Friends of JAM*, would later create the website, www. jeffmartinovich.com, to post defense motions and petitions in an attempt to balance the overwhelming control the prosecution holds on the narrative, as well as the understanding held by the public.

My circle of supporters and I did not understand that while most European and Latin American countries pursue the *inquisitorial* legal system in which the court is charged with *pursuing the truth*, the United States follows the *adversarial* legal system that, contrarily, poses two adversaries in support of *their side* of the case. These adversaries' duties, within the law, are to win their case. Once again, I had convinced myself that if I just got the opportunity to talk to the prosecutors and present my side of the story to the judge and jury, everyone would see how I couldn't have possibly meant any harm! I did not understand that the prosecution's charge was to *not help me* show the truth and lack of intent by myself and my team. Their job was to win. I now find my naiveté almost childish.

I couldn't believe I was charged with twenty-six different allegations of wire fraud, money laundering, and conspiracy. The media often reported I faced over 300 years in federal prison if I were convicted of all charges. All these counts flowed out of a single charge or predicate, as it's called in criminal law, of placing an inflated price on EPV Solar stock and earning that extra $140,000. But what I didn't understand, and I would later learn the jury members didn't understand, was that the final sentencing would normally be the same amount of time if I were found guilty of all twenty-six counts, or just one allegation. This was another critical miscalculation.

Each time I, or anyone in my firm, sent an email, or mailed a report, referencing EPV Solar, or even discussed EPV Solar, a new fraud count could be recorded. The number of counts could have been 10,000.

The charges in *United States v. Martinovich, Criminal No. 4:12cr101* were listed as:

- Count 1—Conspiracy to Commit Mail and Wire Fraud, in violation of Title 18, United States Code, Section 1349. [Talking about EPV Solar valuations]

- Counts 2–9—Wire Fraud, in violation of Title 18, United States Code, Sections 1343. [Sending an email about EPV Solar]

- Counts 10–14—Mail Fraud, in violation of Title 18, United States Code, Sections 1341. [Sending a letter about EPV Solar]

- Counts 15–23—Engaging in Monetary Transaction in Property Derived from Specified Unlawful Activity, in violation of Title 18, United States Code, Sections 1957. [Wiring or ACH'ing transactions ref. EPV Solar]

- Counts 24–26—Fraudulent Oaths and Declarations in Relation to a Bankruptcy Proceeding, in violation of Title 18, United States Code, Section 152 and 2. [Whole other story I'll tell you about!]

When juries are presented with so many charges, human psychology applies deductive reasoning to the different elements, and more times than not finds the defendant guilty on some counts, innocent on others, and as in my case, undecided on more. The deductive reasoning many times supports a juror's conclusion they convicted on certain counts but, also, gave the defendant the benefit of the doubt on other items to, in effect, lessen culpability and punishment. Yet, in federal criminal cases, the jury is not permitted to be informed of the length of sentence each charge may hold. What would they decide if they knew the sentence for one count was normally the same long-term sentence for twenty-six counts?

Defense specialists explain this phenomenon accounts for the prosecution's tactic of overcharging to increase the odds of the expected conviction and sentence on at least one charge.

After four grueling weeks, the jury would later find me guilty on seventeen counts, not guilty on three counts, and undecided on five counts. [Doc. 92, Dtd 5/07/2013]

Entering this trial, the fundamental charge against me, fraud, carried a crucial element of intent. By definition, the prosecution must prove, and the jury must believe, the defendant *intentionally* committed the acts that caused harm.

I was terrified we had missed some piece of evidence that actually did show wrongdoing, but I convinced myself there was no way anyone would ever believe I *intentionally* caused harm. As most leaders reading this story understand, I never once through these challenges had that "pit in the bottom of my stomach feeling" that I, or my team, had done anything wrong, or unethical, or, certainly, criminal. That lack of doubt gave me the false confidence we were entering a proceeding to uncover the truth. Yet, we were entering a war of adversaries and I, and my warriors, were greatly outmatched in *The Art of War*.

When considering integrity, a leader will likely identify with the definition of "the quality of being honest and having strong moral principles." Yet when facing extreme adversity, leaders should consider the secondary definition as "the state of being whole and undivided." Character and integrity many times are no match for resourceful adversaries who may align multiple estates in unison. Leaders must prepare to combat their adversity on multiple fronts, simultaneously, in order to navigate a path to victory.

The Trial Begins

On April 10, 2013, my trial began in the US District Court, Eastern District of Virginia, before the Honorable Judge Robert Doumar. In his opening statement, AUSA Brian Samuels laid out for the jury the government's theory of the case:

- "The defendant executed a lengthy and complex fraud by enticing investors to put their money into a hedge fund [Martinovich] solely controlled through the use of false representations and omissions."

- "Falsely inflating the value of the assets and the hedge fund to serve his own ends ...."

- "Martinovich developed a lavish exorbitant lifestyle ...."

- "Rather than obtain independent valuations of the venture funds assets ... Martinovich doubled the value of the EPV solar shares ... because Martinovich wanted to take a substantial fund management fee ...."

- "The incentive fee served as a needed injection of cash ... increases that were rubber stamped by the so-called valuation expert."

The central part of the testimony concerned the allegations I forced everyone to misprice the value of our position in EPV Solar, the solar energy company at the heart of the government's case against me, and that I did so in order to earn $140,000 more in management fees, on top of the $8,000,000 in fees we legally earned that period.

Sample Testimony

After I was indicted, two junior brokers on my advisory team capitalized on my disarray and snared as many former clients as possible from my personal book of business. Jayne DiVincenzo and Jennifer Daknis resigned from MICG Investment Management, transferring to an independent broker-dealer, Linsco Private Ledger (LPL), and taking a number of clients with them. Linsco paid commission rates up to 90 percent, while advisors at MICG received 40–50 percent of the advisory fees.

Both testified against me in the trial, not identifying any evidence of wrongdoing but, definitely, piling on the character assassination, which, ultimately, proved ample for the jury. The dialogue with the government was well-practiced and extremely effective.

US Attorney Dougherty: And did you notice any changes in Mr. Martinovich during your time at MICG?

Ms. DiVincenzo: Sadly, yes.

US Attorney Dougherty: Tell us about those.

Ms. DiVincenzo: In my first two years at the firm I think he was one of the best managers I've ever had.

US Attorney Dougherty: Why?

Ms. DiVincenzo: Mr. Martinovich was—he's probably the best salesman I've ever been around. He's optimistic, positive, and doesn't say derogatory things. You know, he was always very good, again, at sales. Clients loved him. His—a lot of his team members, like myself, were huge fans.

And then I'm not really sure what precipitated the change, but—I don't know if Mr. Martinovich started to believe his own press, but he thought he was immortal and seemed to be spending more than he should be for what our revenues were, maintaining a show, a lifestyle, that just seemed incongruent with, you know, what the economy was doing. Not very good at accepting criticism or feedback.

One opportunity I had to express concerns to Mr. Martinovich was at 9:30 in the morning at the Marriott Hotel. He was drinking Sauvignon Blanc at 9:30 in the morning. I mentioned to him I was very concerned that he might have a drinking problem, and he blew up at me. And I knew my days were numbered there. [Tr. p. 1186]

Following the testimony of Jayne DiVincenzo, Jennifer Daknis took the stand.

US Attorney Dougherty: Did you lose any clients on the basis of Mr. Martinovich's behavior?

Ms. Daknis: Yes.

US Attorney Dougherty: What specific clients?

Ms. Daknis: I lost probably two or three clients around the summer of '08 because of his affair on his wife! [Tr. p. 1531].

I had recruited Keith Reagan and Clayton James, a financial advisory team from Merrill Lynch, and as the custom had paid them hundreds of thousands of dollars in forgivable loans to transfer their book of business and hit certain revenue targets with MICG Investment Management. Keith and Clayton, subsequently, had never met these agreed-upon targets and were in significant debt on our books. So I was not surprised to see them take their places and testify against me.

US Attorney Samuels: *Do you recall with some specificity Mr. Martinovich's response?*

Clayton James: *I think the response was something like, you know, "Goddammit, Reagan. Why are you f---ing calling me asking me about these f---ing hedge funds? It's none of your f---ing business where I come up with these valuations. You need to go f---ing do what you f---ing said you're going to do, and quit f---ing calling me, asking me about these funds." He went on to say, "You guys haven't f---ing done what you f---ing said you're going to do. You need to get off your f---ing ass and go f---ing do what you f---ing said you were going to do and quit calling me asking me about these f---ing funds."*

US Attorney Samuels: *Had you ever had this type of conversation or treatment by Mr. Martinovich before?*

Clayton James: *No.*

Given that my team and I grew MICG Investment Management from zero to over a billion dollars brick-by-brick, I took each testimony as a personal loss and betrayal. Our families had raised children together, vacationed together, and enjoyed the fruits of success. Our associates truly were a team, unlike most organizations that use this term as an aspirational goal. We had built a unique A-Player culture, which on top of providing the best-available investment service to our clients promoted an environment of friendly competition, committed community service, and a place where everyone else wanted to come to work. We turned down 99 percent of applicants for positions. MICG people were valued by the region for the firm's commitment to the community and charity events, and unlike most corporate colloquiums, MICG truly was a very special place and recognized as such by all stakeholders.

Prosecution Strategy

The prosecution had to overcome and counteract the substantial good works performed by the company and myself in the previous two decades. My own participation had to be erased. I had served as president of Big Brothers Big Sisters, chairman of The Children's Village, board director for the USO, and so many more positions, along with an open checkbook for pretty much every community leader who had a worthy initiative.

The government cleverly stipulated that I did good work, but then attempted to negate everything by painting me as a wealthy, narcissistic, gambling, womanizing, alcoholic CEO who finally went off the rails after the Financial Crisis of 2008. This was the only way these fraudulent, inconsistent behaviors could be believed by a jury. The strategy helped the jurors overcome what would otherwise be a debilitating case of cognitive dissonance—*the state of having inconsistent thoughts, beliefs, or attitudes, especially as relating to behavioral decisions and attitude change.* They were brilliant. Netflix could not have presented a more binge-worthy series.

I struggled to objectively understand everyone's scramble to protect their own self-interests and to capitalize on the opportunity offered by my vulnerable state. The takeaway: *never let a good crisis go to waste.* The testimonies were incredibly well-scripted. In the courtroom I could see the prosecution guide each new witness into the conference room behind the observers. I imagined the prosecution team carefully rehearsing each testimony.

The narrative was hammered home along with a superb case of class warfare just in case any hard-working Newport News, Virginia, juror hadn't been paying attention. On the large courtroom monitors, AUSA Brian Samuels would repeatedly display pictures of my conspicuous consumption: Ferrari, Bentley, and beach house. These displays of excess became common topics of the prosecution, newspapers, and even occupying twenty minutes of Judge Doumar's sentencing soliloquy.

There is a leadership lesson here. How many CEOs and entrepreneurs reading this are right now taking inventory of what will be turned against them once the extreme adversity arrives?

I take a small measure of satisfaction in knowing that the jury originally signaled the judge they could not reach a consensus on any of the charges. According to some media reports based on interviews with members of the jury after the trial ended, three members of the jury believed the government failed to provide any evidence of my criminality. Nevertheless, Judge Doumar refused to accept that the trial would end with a hung jury and a mistrial. It was late on a Friday afternoon and the Judge instructed the exhausted jury to return again Monday morning to restart deliberations. Monday, after three hours, the jury announced they were ready to deliver a unanimous verdict. Guilty. Now the jury could go home to their families and resume their lives.

Following the trial, the jury forewoman would state to *The Daily Press*, discarding the fact of my divorce, "He took two women to Las Vegas, and neither one of them was named Mrs. Martinovich" [Daily

Press, Peter Dujardin, July 21, 2013]. My friends would ask, "And what does this have to do with a stock price in a hedge fund?"

Leadership Failure

Yet, this theater aside, my failure to protect the firm, and making so many poor decisions when faced with our black swan, was the true betrayal and the fundamental source of my difficulties. All the people around me—employees, clients, partners, shareholders—had confidence in me to lead them through good times and bad. They trusted me with their careers and security, and I never once considered I would let it all disappear. At the end, their confidence in me was misplaced. I was not strong enough.

> Integrity demands responsibility. When faced with adversity, great leaders must take the responsibility to make good on the contract entrusted to us by our employees, shareholders, and family. We have to perform at these most critical moments, put the interests of our beneficiaries ahead of our own, and do whatever it takes to lead those put in our charge to calmer waters.

The one piece of solace I do have is the incredible, continued success the great majority of MICG team members have gone on to experience during the decade I have been battling incarceration, reversing US District Court rulings, and watching two US federal judges removed from my case. Almost to a person, they have remained in the financial industry, continued to grow significant businesses, and lead consequential lives. I often try to coach myself up by considering how I played a significant role in introducing these excellent people to the business and developing their industry knowledge and skill sets. In an ironic twist, I instilled in them the strong character and integrity necessary to build great careers for themselves, even if they may, very possibly, now believe differently in me.

Extreme adversity so clearly highlights the demarcation line many times between caring for ourselves and making sure our employees, or even our children, are going to be okay. If we have invested great time, energy, and resources into their knowledge, attitudes, and overachieving culture, they will grow up to be fine without us. Our finest achievement is for them *not* to need us, especially when we make the incredible mistakes I have.

CHAPTER 7

SEEING WHAT'S BARELY VISIBLE

You talk about seeing around corners as an element of success. That's what differentiates the good leader. Not many people have it. Not many people can predict that corner. That would be a characteristic of great leaders.

—JACK WELCH, CEO, GENERAL ELECTRIC

I SPENT A CAREER ADVISING CLIENTS how to protect their assets, diversify their investments, and plan for rainy days. The irony is that I ended up being the poster child for unpreparedness.

Beyond the trauma of the events that sent me to prison, it is incredibly embarrassing how dumb I was in regard to protecting our company, our employees, our shareholders, and, of course, my personal assets and my family's security. I had 20-20 vision for seeing what was right in front of me for everyone we helped, but I was blindsided by the barely visible when it came to my own destiny.

As many overburdened and overextended leaders can relate, I rarely reviewed the financing closing documents, the voluminous trust paperwork, the audit disclaimers, or the legal engagement letters. I had a team of advisors to read documents. I was a leader who delegated. They told me that was good!

But I never considered—and I should have—that my signatures on documents and personal guarantees would come back to destroy everything I worked for and devour the assets I had so carefully constructed for our employees, shareholders, and my family.

I had too much confidence in the limited liability entities, holding companies, and intricate corporate structures my attorneys and accountants assured me would protect our assets. As it happened, regulators easily pierced all the veils and swapped millions of dollars from the Assets column to the Liabilities column on our balance sheet.

Too Much Trust

I put too much trust in the army of attorneys I hired to defend me against the type of adversity I was facing, and I was too weak to take back the responsibility myself for correcting the failures I had put in place. I never anticipated that as soon as I was under federal investigation, all the lawyers on my team would scatter like cockroaches when the kitchen light was flicked on. One by one they either withdrew or ghosted me in a manner I never imagined could happen. I suppose the lawyers concluded I didn't have much of a chance and their own career prospects would be better served by representing clients who needed LLC documents updated or new registered agents filed for their Wyoming organization.

Many nights through the investigation, indictment, and trial, I imagined all the lawyers and accountants meeting up at Todd Jurich's Bistro in Norfolk, Virginia, and raising drinks at my expense. Everyone knew what was coming and where the bread was buttered, except me. Throughout my career, I always had an irrational fear I would die a young man with my tombstone reading, *Not nearly as smart as we thought he was.* My fear was not irrational.

> To overcome extreme adversity, leaders must prepare for the disaster well before it arrives. Asset protection strategies must be set in place now. Noah built the Ark before he felt one drop of rain.

I had personally guaranteed our company financing and obligations, as nearly all entrepreneurs and business leaders must do until their organizations reach significant asset levels. I could have shifted this burden away from my personal balance sheet numerous times. I knew what to do. I just never got around to it.

Worst of all, I had zero fear this was even an issue. I had set up a sophisticated family trust that took care of everyone and minimized taxes. That's the good news. The bad news is that I never implemented an irrevocable asset protection structure that would have preserved the financial security of my family. Another good thing I did was buy life insurance. The policy would pay my estate $13 million at my death. More than once I lamented the fact that the adversity I faced took everything from me but my life. Many nights I thought my family would have been better off without me. Of course, I could not continue these premium payments, and this benefit to my family was also erased.

> Policies, protocols, and people need to be set with a view to what is the worst that could happen. Hope is not a strategy. Blind optimism is not a strategy. I urge all leaders to reassess their own vulnerability in the same manner the US military constantly war games scenario after scenario of terrible events befalling the country.

Here Comes the Judge Again

My lack of preparedness made me the sitting duck for the regulators and the prosecutors. But I was most unprepared for the courtroom experience led by the Honorable Robert Doumar of the US District Court for the Eastern District of Virginia.

Doumar was born in Norfolk in February 1930. He was active in Republican politics and co-managed Richard Nixon's Norfolk campaigns in 1968 and 1972. He was a delegate to the Republican National Convention in 1968, 1972, and 1976 where he met California Governor Ronald Reagan. After Reagan became president in 1980, Virginia Senator John Warner, a law school classmate, sponsored Doumar for the federal bench. On November 5, 1981, President Reagan nominated Doumar to a seat on the US District Court for the Eastern District of Virginia, and he was confirmed by the Senate on December 3, 1981.

As recounted in chapter 4, my first encounter with the eighty-three-year-old Judge Doumar was at a hearing to postpone the trial due to my father's hospice condition. The judge was prepared to make an example of me even if the request for extension was from the government. It appeared that my guilt was a foregone conclusion and I would have to begin to overcome a paradigm of *guilt before proven innocent.*

I have to admit I was forewarned by my attorney, James Broccoletti, about the "feistiness" of Judge Doumar. Broccoletti told me, "Watch how terribly the judge treats me, and he likes me the best! He actually selects me for difficult cases." But I was not prepared for the uphill battle to present our defense, as well as the influence the Judge's perception of the case and demeanor to the prosecution and defense had on the proceedings and ultimate outcome.

Since this experience, in the news I have closely followed the tremendous impact the Judge's beliefs and politics have on the courtroom outcome. I naively believed they would be an impartial arbiter who simply administrated the case, but learned they are the most influential role player in the outcome. Later when we reached out to attorney Sidney Powell to possibly represent my appeal I was shocked at her first questions. "Who appointed the judge? Is he conservative or liberal?"

Uphill Battle

In an attempt to enlighten our readers as to the uphill battle they may face when confronting their own extreme adversity, I will simply provide the court records here.

Judge Doumar did not buy the auditor's repeated declarations that he believed EPV Solar was priced correctly:

> "When the critical defense witness, independent hedge fund auditor Mr. Umscheid, asserted that he had vetted the stock valuation reports and valuation expert, as well as personally approved and supported the questioned $2.88 stock price, Judge Doumar rose from his chair, ordered the jury out of

the courtroom, and berated Mr. Umscheid on the perils of perjury. When the jury returned, the key witness was clearly intimidated and discredited in the eyes of the jury." [Tr. p. 2453]

Judge Doumar did not believe the government's star witness, J. Peter Lynch, provided a credible valuation report in New York City:

"When key government witness, independent solar valuation expert Mr. Lynch, asserted that he had prepared the valuation reports, he had placed his signature directly below the questioned $2.88 stock price, and he believed that at that time it was a conservative valuation price, Judge Doumar attempted to now discredit the failed government witness by yelling in front of the jury, 'So your appraisal is absolutely worthless.'" [Tr. p.487]

Judge Doumar wanted to communicate his opinion of the valuations to the media:

"Prior to deliberation, with the non-sequestered jury having access to *The Daily Press*, the local newspaper provided the jurors with Judge Doumar's statements in front of the media, 'There isn't a scintilla—a scintilla of evidence that there was any reason to raise the value $2.15 to $2.88, not a single thing.'"[2] [Tr. p.3237]

I had a difficult time explaining my side of the narrative while being interrupted 168 times by the presiding judge:

"Court-appointed appeal counsel, Mr. Woodward, submitted that Judge Doumar interrupted and interfered with Mr. Martinovich's personal testimony a shocking 168 times." [Case No. 13-4828]

Shockingly, Judge Doumar even objected in place of the prosecution:

"During counsel's questioning of defense witness Mr. Umscheid, Judge Doumar totally usurped the role of the prosecutor."

BROCCOLETTI: "Did you consider the stock market crash of just a couple months before that?"

UMSCHEID: "Well, remember the reason—"

COURT: Objection(!)

Judge Doumar surprisingly objected in place of AUSA Samuels. [Tr. p.2536]

Mr. Brian Samuels, AUSA, was greatly concerned himself this proceeding would quickly end in a mistrial:

"AUSA Mr. Samuels, himself, counseled Judge Doumar to hopefully prevent a mistrial. Mr. Samuels stated, 'Judge, given the court's comments and concerns…I just want to be certain that the record is clear that we will raise and object to the concerns…I just don't want there to be any issue with this down the road, so I don't' feel it's incumbent on us as the government to attempt to protect the record.'" [Tr. p.2529] [USCA4 Appeal: 19-6797 Doc: 4-1 Filed: 06/06/2019]

More descriptive and conclusive, I will simply list the quotations from the Fourth Circuit Court of Appeals Order, written by Circuit Judges Duncan, Diaz, and Davis, describing the challenges a leader may be presented with if deciding to stand up for his company, employees, shareholders, and family [No. 13-4828, Doc. 214, Dtd. 01/07/2016]:

- "(I)n light of the district court's demeanor at trial and its statements during sentencing regarding the nature of the guidelines it is necessary for a different judge to be assigned to this matter."

- "(T)he district court's actions were in error."

- "Interference in this case went beyond the pale."

- "The district court became so disruptive that it impermissibly interfered with the manner in which appellant sought to present his evidence."

- "We agree that the district court crossed the line and was in error."

- "The district court unnecessarily interrupted defense counsel's presentation of the defense at trial."

- "The district court's general interference in defendant's trial—which included examining witnesses, interrupting counsel, and controlling the presentation—strayed too far."

- "Here, there was much more than an appearance of improper interference."

- "Considering the breadth of the district court's actions, from questioning witnesses and counsel to interrupting unnecessarily, we find the district court strayed too far from convention."

- "At some point, repeated injudicious conduct must be recognized by this Court as a compelling basis for finding plain error."

Another Bite at the Apple

Having the Appeals Court recognize Judge Doumar's oversight of a bizarre trial was a short-lived victory for me. The good news is that Judge Doumar was removed. The bad news is that the Fourth Circuit Court of Appeals, although consuming page after page of almost unheard-of reprimand and rebuke of a trial judge, stated nonetheless that, due to defense attorney James Broccoletti's error to never once object to the "interference in this case (that) went beyond the pale," they could not reverse the conviction and could not permit a new, fair trial. My conviction would stand.

My goose was cooked and if I believed the court, I had no one to blame but my own attorney and, of course, myself. I have been asked many times why James Broccoletti, a seasoned federal defense attorney with the hourly rates to prove it, never once raised an objection to the clearly bizarre and unreasonable proceedings of the trial. It would be improper, and unprofessional, of me to speculate why he did not preserve our opportunity for a new, fair trial. My family, friends, and associates certainly have their own strong opinions. It remains an enigma, and he remains an enigma. Possibly, one day I may have an opportunity to ask him.

The education was too late for me, but I eventually learned that when an attorney fails to object to illegal or improper conduct in court proceedings, this failure makes it almost impossible for an Appeals Court to conclude there was "plain error." Every law student knows that to preserve an error for review and correction on appeal in federal court, a party must make a "specific contemporaneous objection" to the perceived error. A specific contemporaneous objection means the objection must be made immediately after, or very shortly after, the error occurs and it must specifically address the perceived error. This rule is reflected in Federal Rule of Evidence 103. Failing to do so can have disastrous consequences.

That's what happened to me. I found out, too late, that a party that fails to preserve an error for appeal will be prevented from raising the error as a basis for appeal. Of course, again, going into this adventure I had no idea of these rules. Because of my attorney's failure to simply object, the Fourth Circuit Court of Appeals stated, "In light of plain error standard of review . . . we may not intervene" [Doc. 214, Dtd. 01/07/2016]. My conviction would stand.

The challenges leaders will face, when not if, come with what seems like a never-ending pummeling of mishaps and tragedies that cause us to think this must be impossible. But soon, after so many repeated setbacks, we begin to accept them as simply part of our journey in the grand design. And this acceptance, again, helps us to aspire to more strength, intellect, and emotional stability. These strengths then empower us to find that path to survival, and possibly even victory.

As leaders confronted with extreme adversity, we must aspire to more. We must throw aside all excuses of "this is not fair" or "they owe me because I have been so successful." The forces may align against us with overwhelming strength and control, but we must *play the cards we are dealt*. To rage against the system, or the universe, only furthers our decline into self-pity and victimhood. This guarantees defeat. We must accept what we feel is wrong and unfair and focus all our energy and intellect on overcoming what, to us, feels greatly unjust.

See What's Barely Visible

Adversity is disguised in the barely visible. I wish I had invested more of my leadership bandwidth into seeing the forces operating just beneath the surface. Alas, like many leaders, I was hyper-focused on what was front and center: the next thing on my never-ending to-do list. I hardly noticed that events were developing on the periphery.

Like many entrepreneurs, I thrived on change like opening new offices, making great hires, or creating new lines of business I could monetize.

But to the extent I limited my scope to what was visible, I failed to protect the organization and myself from the adversity that was gathering destructive power just under my radar. There was a black swan event just below the horizon and because I failed to look for what's barely visible, I failed to prepare for it.

Black swans don't emit loud quacks, flap their wings, or call attention to themselves. By definition, these events don't announce themselves until it's too late. Again, according to Nassim Taleb, first, they're an outlier. Nothing in the past points to its possibility so it is far outside the realm of the routine. Second, a black swan event is accompanied by far-reaching consequences and extreme impact. Third, there is something about these events that despite being unpredictable, people can't resist making up stories after the fact to explain why they were predictable after all.

Adversity taught me that true leadership calls for knowing where to look and, fundamentally, changing *how* leaders see. When adversity threatens, leaders who develop clearer peripheral vision are better positioned to navigate uncertainty. Peripheral vision is the ability to see objects, threats, and opportunities just outside your direct line of vision, and as a former point guard, I should have possessed much greater vision.

Making the invisible visible is one of the superpowers I should have developed. I would have been better able to recognize the threat, develop responses, and have the clarity of vision to construct bulwarks and strategies to minimize the impacts of the adversity on my business, shareholders, and family. It would have enabled me to write a new script adapted to respond to the unwelcome reality unfolding before me. Leadership is the ability to see new conditions emerging on the horizon and to respond with novel strategies adapted to these new conditions. If that's not an actionable definition of effective leadership, I don't know what is.

Finally, the federal criminal justice system provides another path meant to remedy the effects and sometimes devastating consequences from judges taking the law into their own hands. It is identified as The Judicial Conduct and Disability Act of 1980, 28 U.S.C. §§ 351–364. It established a process by which any person can file a complaint alleging a federal judge has engaged in "conduct prejudicial to the effective and expeditious administration of the business of the courts" or has become, by reason of a mental or physical disability, "unable to discharge all the duties" of the judicial office.

Unfortunately, similar to the laws prohibiting cameras and audio recordings in federal courtrooms, The Judicial Conduct and Disability Act also includes an opaque set of confidentiality interpretations for the proceedings. Cases noting further incarceration for speaking of these rulings are available to review in the federal record. The discovery of these provisions, again, in the United States of America made no sense to me.

Confidentiality of Proceedings. Except as provided in section 355, all papers, documents, and records of proceedings related to investigations conducted under this chapter shall be confidential and shall not be disclosed by any person in any proceeding except to the extent that—

> (1) the judicial council of the circuit in its discretion releases a copy of a report of a special committee under section 353(c) to the complainant whose complaint initiated the investigation by that special committee and to the judge whose conduct is the subject of the complaint;

If an Order is released by the Court of Appeals sanctioning a federal judge, it does not include any identifying criteria of the judge's name, the case number, or the defendant's name. It is only identified by a number, and this number is publicly listed on the court of appeal's website, because everything must be "public." But you could only find the Order if you knew the number. And if you knew the number, then did someone publicly disclose this proceeding so you would know the number?

> *Public Availability of Written Orders.* Each written order to implement any action under section 354(a)(1)(C), which is issued by a judicial council, the Judicial Conference, or the standing committee established under section 331, shall be made available to the public through the appropriate clerk's office of the court of appeals for the circuit. Unless contrary to the interests of justice, each such order shall be accompanied by written reasons therefor. [28 U.S. Code § 360(b)]

Also, according to these statutes, the issue may be resolved if the chief judge of the Appeals Court "determines that the subject judge has taken appropriate voluntary corrective action that acknowledges and remedies the problems raised by the complaint" [Jud. Conduct R.

11(d)(2)]. "(A)ppropriate corrective action for conduct that resulted in identifiable, particularized harm should include steps taken to acknowledge and redress the harm, if possible, such as by an apology, recusal from a case, or a pledge to refrain from similar conduct in the future" [Jud. Conduct R. 11 cmt.].

If at the time of my trial and appeal, I had filed a Judicial Complaint, and *if* the Fourth Circuit Court of Appeals Chief Judge, Judge Roger L. Gregory at the time, had written a Memorandum and Order with regard to apologies and corrective action, what would be a very rare occurrence at any time, then I believe I could not even now admit there had been such an Order.

Because it wouldn't matter, anyways. Even if there had been an Order and everyone apologized for severe misconduct and devastating harm to all stakeholders, the conviction was never reversed, a new trial was never granted, and our employees, shareholders, and families never had the opportunity to rebuild and restore.

> **Overcoming great adversity requires pragmatic, solutions-oriented efforts applied over and over until achieving final victory. More times than not, the paths we feel will be productive are not, and the outlier efforts in which we had little faith come through for us. Therefore, daily, exhaustive, productive actions are mandatory in order to even have a chance at survival. Failure is not an option.**

RUNNING *TO* PRISON

AT 4:16 ON THE AFTERNOON of November 12, 2013, my attorney James Broccoletti called. "I'm sorry, Jeff. Your bond has been denied. You have to report to Morgantown Federal Prison by noon tomorrow. Don't be late!"

To spare my family further embarrassment and pain, I decided to drive myself to prison. For readers who may be facing a similar requirement, let me be upfront: don't make the mistake I did. You can't show up in prison with a car. Most people get a ride or take a taxi. I wasn't thinking. The prospect of prison will do that to you.

So at 3 a.m., I left Newport News in my Audi and started the 382-mile drive to Morgantown, West Virginia. I figured it would take me six to seven hours, plenty of time to report by noon. Without thinking about it too much, I asked the Siri voice assistant to guide me. In the darkness of the night, I started dictating increasingly desperate messages to the few friends still speaking to me.

"Kevin, I'm driving myself to prison, better find a new partner for the Member-Guest tourney."

"Sean, never ever, ever invest in a solar company!"

"Dave, never hire a defense attorney whose name sounds like a vegetable nobody likes!"

By 8 a.m., I was in West Virginia. I think. The morning fog made reading the road signs difficult on the winding roads. Siri was becoming less and less dependable as cellular service faded in and out. I looked for a roadside tavern. I urgently needed a drink. But then I remembered one piece of advice from Broccoletti. He said the second thing they do to new inmates is make them take a breathalyzer test. The first thing is a full body cavity search.

Then Siri died! Why did I not print out driving directions? Why did I not remember to bring a charger? I didn't know where I was. Time was getting short, and my blood pressure was rising. "Just keep it together," I whispered to myself. It was all I could do to keep the car in the proper lane along the frog-shrouded winding roads.

I finally got to Morgantown and found a corner diner. It was past 11 a.m. Plows had lined the shoulders of the road with coal-dirty snow. The diner parking lot was treacherous with slush.

No time for even a cup of coffee. Behind the counter stood a pierced and tattooed server with a name badge that said "Darlene." I don't know who I was kidding when I said, "Darlene … I have a meeting at the Morgantown Federal Prison at noon today. May I trouble you for directions?"

She sized me up twice in my Hugo Boss sport coat and Gucci loafers. She knew what noon meant. Still, she took pity on me. "It ain't far." Darlene pointed a tobacco-stained finger out the window. "Mile and a half down that road."

Now time was running short. I turned into the prison entrance and pulled up to the guard shack with all the military composure I could muster.

"Jeff Martinovich reporting, Sir!"

The burly guard waddled over. He looked like a Kentucky bourbon barrel with a beard. He leaned onto the car door scanning the situation, looking from the passenger seat to the back seat to see where the other driver was.

"You done drove yourself to prison?"

"Long story, Sir. I'll just park over there and my buddy, Mike, will pick up the car tomorrow."

He looked at me like I'd lost my mind, spit some type of juice on my front left tire (I swear!), and bellowed, "You ain't parking here. Back to town and taxi back is your only option. You got half an hour, or you'll be starting your sentence in the Hole!"

I wasn't sure what the hole was, but the way he capitalized it, I was sure it wasn't anything good. Now driving frantically back to the diner, I knew that getting a taxi out here would be futile. Darlene! My only hope! I ran in.

"Uh, Darlene, I didn't exactly give you the whole story earlier. If I don't report to prison in ... I checked my Seiko ... 16 minutes ... they're going to throw me in the hole! Could I talk you into driving me? You can drive the Audi!" Hell, at that moment I was willing to give her the Audi.

This was my first experience of how my new identity as a felon would be regarded. Darlene took two dramatic steps back, making it clear this would not be a possibility.

There was only one thing to do. I left my car in the diner parking lot, tossed my phone, watch, wallet, and keys into the glove box, slammed the door, looked to the sky, and started running through the slush. "Okay, God," I yelled to the sky now beginning to snow. "If this is the way it has to be, then this is the way it has to be!"

I ran across the slushy parking lot, dodging cars through the intersection and into a full sprint against traffic alongside county highway 857. The shoulder was deep with plowed snow, I was too terrified to be cold, and a constant stream of F-150s battered me with spray. The drivers were baffled by this lunatic running for his life in loafers!

I wasn't going to make it. A second talk with God. "After all this you have to let me make it!" Then a sudden break in traffic. I swerved onto the pavement and channeled the best Chariots of Fire my forty-seven-year-old body could summon.

The next thing I knew, I was through the gate, clutching my knees, soaked to the bone, gasping. I heard "Two minutes to spare. Never thought you'd make it."

There would be no hole today for prisoner 81091-083!

CHAPTER 8

PRACTICE HUMILITY

Do you wish to rise? Begin by descending.

You plan a tower that will pierce the clouds?

Lay first the foundation of humility.

—SAINT AUGUSTINE

WHEN AFTER CONSIDERABLE STRUGGLES one becomes fortunate to achieve financial and career success, practicing humility becomes almost a full-time job. With each year of ever-expanding achievement, I increasingly misplaced my priorities. If humility means not thinking less of yourself but thinking of yourself less often, I definitely lost my way. My attention increasingly focused on the things that money can buy: fine suits, fine cars, private jet travel, and the Chihuly chandelier for the foyer. And, in turn, I, ever so slowly, stopped prioritizing beating everyone to the office and showing up at the 6 a.m. workouts that made me so productive.

Now, let me pause here and stress I do not buy into the crowd that says you have to drive a Buick (sorry, Tiger!) and buy cheap suits so your clients don't think you make too much money providing their services. On the contrary, I subscribe 100 percent to the school of thought that successful people want to work with successful people. As long as you join those circles with the right attitude and balance of values, it can be an effective business strategy. It is easy for everyone to believe the *Wolf of Wall Street* stereotype because it feeds human insecurities and our excuse-driven culture. Yet, the great majority of successful, and wealthy, people I have come to know in my own success have been kind, generous, and humble. Many acquired their wealth as first-generation entrepreneurs and honored their humble beginnings by not flaunting their success.

But I kept slipping, and I served up so many symbols and narratives my detractors could use against me, in business as well as the legal battle I was too blind to see waiting to ambush me. One symbol was membership in the James River Country Club, not because of exorbitant dues but because of the selective acceptance process. On Friday afternoons, I participated in the golf scramble. I rationalized doing so brought our firm more business as I hobnobbed with the who's who of our small business community. My son, Cole, would later laugh with me at the young trust fund sons telling me each evening about how I should run my business and invest for our clients.

My purchase of a Bentley automobile was another way I signaled my success. Little did I know it also signaled my obliviousness to how it looked and how it would be used against me. Sarah, a friend and long-term club member, was not happy with my conspicuous consumption. She pulled me aside, like the principal pulling a student by the ear, and whispered, "Are you crazy buying a brand-new Bentley? In Newport News, Virginia?!"

"But it's not the big fancy model!" I lamely protested.

"You just don't get it," she said. "They will crucify you for this."
And she was right.

At the time, though, the exchange seemed ludicrous to me.
I ordered another martini from the bartender, Bob, and quickly
dismissed the conversation, like I dismissed most conversations that
threatened to confront me with reality.

Not long after that conversation, I had to endure another conversation. Actually it was more of a lecture. US Federal District Judge,
The Honorable Robert A. Doumar, addressed the packed courtroom
and the gallery of reporters.

"I don't know that I've ever seen a Bentley," the judge began.
"I've seen lots of Rolls Royces. So Mr. Martinovich—I've never seen
him drive around in that Bentley . . . don't think Frank Batten, who
was the richest man in this area, ever drove a Bentley or a Maserati,
at least not one that anybody around here ever saw. The defendant
built an excessive and lavish lifestyle on the backs of his victims' hard
work and savings. That Bentley, that Maserati, that house on the
James River, those trips to Vegas, the Christmas parties, the luxury
everything—all that was built on the lies he told to people who trusted
him." [Sentencing Tr. p. 14,76]

> If we have the foresight to arrange our lives today in prepa-
> ration for not only continued success but also in anticipation
> for extreme adversity that will likely appear, our chances of
> survival will increase dramatically. If I had practiced greater
> humility in my material acquisitions, as well as my lifestyle
> and personal choices, I would have likely fared much better
> in my challenges with regulators, shareholders, and jurors.

RIOT 101

I certainly was getting daily lessons in humility while I focused on survival at FCI Fort Dix, New Jersey. Four thousand Bloods, Crips, Latin Kings, and *Chomos* forced me to navigate my day with extreme awareness and focus. The key was not to be subservient, because then you became someone's *bitch*, but to balance humility and strength while maintaining a fragile détente with your potential attackers.

One Saturday morning in the fall of 2014, I awoke early in my twelve-man room to prepare my legal work and make the 8:00 a.m. bell when they opened our building doors for *the move*. I had 10 minutes to make my way to the next location. I threw on my gray prison sweats because I wanted to get a quick run in at the track before spending the day in the law library. I heard yelling and swearing in the room next door followed by loud thuds against the wall and banging of metal bunks, a regular fight that barely went noticed. I would later learn that Jose, of the Puerto Rican gang, had refused to pay back Hector, of the Mexican gang, a book of stamps that was prison currency.

As I circled the track, the 9:00 a.m. bell rang and the doors to the buildings all opened with a stream of nearly one hundred members of the Puerto Rican and Mexican gangs sprinting toward me, everyone holding a knife or shank high in the air, some as long as swords. Like a scene from the Scottish battlefields in *Braveheart*, the prisoners ran at each other and clashed in violent struggles stabbing each other all around me. I watched in amazement as Jose grabbed the top of a six-foot fence and vaulted into the next zone. Prisoner after prisoner vaulted after him while never dropping their knives. I grabbed my book bag with my stack of current motions and held it in front of me bouncing off attackers as I kept my head on a swivel. Fortunately, I didn't appear to be a target, but I didn't want to catch an indiscriminate swing of the blade, prematurely ending my own battle.

I shuffled from the center of the track toward the side gates, keeping my bag in front for protection, with time seeming to move in slow motion and the distance to safety seeming insurmountable. After what felt like a lifetime, I slipped through the end gate just as the prison guards in riot gear entered the track and began clubbing inmates and subduing the crowd. I sprinted back to my building before all the doors were locked and I would have been left outside to be identified as a rioter. I kept sprinting upstairs back to my room and jumped under the covers in my rear corner bunk since a standing count would be coming soon to identify the guilty missing parties.

My corner bunk window in Building 5802 overlooked the medical facility where many days I would watch inmates wheeled out to ambulances and guards smoking without urgency. If someone had a heart attack, or was stabbed, the compound would go on *lockdown* so the ambulance was safe to enter the facility. This process normally took forty-five minutes, and we knew any heart attack victim, or recipient of a significant shank, had little chance of survival by the time they eventually made it to a hospital.

I regularly watched stretchers being rolled out with the sheets covering the occupants' heads. I could never reconcile these observations with the relatively low number of official deaths of inmates reported by the Bureau of Prisons. The disparity between my observations and the official records was generally explained to me by the fact that inmates are declared dead only at the hospital so their deaths are not counted against the prison. I cannot attest to the correct answer.

Sometimes adversity can require extreme humility and basic survival instincts just to be able to remain alive long enough to find a path to victory. As crazy as it may sound during comfortable times, first focusing on staying alive may become the primary objective without which nothing else is possible. Mentally and physically, we must become as clever and strong as possible to not take our own lives, as a number of my associates had in the wake of the 2008 Financial Crisis, and to not let violence, disease, or fatal maladies destroy us before we are able to rise from the ashes.

Miracle #1

And then I received a love letter. Ashleigh worked in MICG Investment Management as a young mortgage loan officer with our Lending Division. Fresh out of Old Dominion University, her five-foot stature paled against her incredible energy, personality, and drive to succeed. I admit I saw much of my early self in her positive efforts, and I likely gave her a little more attention to help ensure she succeeded in her job. And Ashleigh knocked it out of the park. She exceeded every milestone we set together.

Within two weeks of every new MICG teammate starting work with the firm, they would be scheduled a three-hour session with me to learn about MICG corporate culture, colloquially called the MICG Kool-Aid. Yes, Ashleigh drank the Kool-Aid (we later had to change it to "The MICG Special Sauce") almost more than anyone else.

This meeting might have involved just one new employee, or as many as three or four recent hires if we had had a busy recruiting month. It was part of our onboarding process. New employees had to suffer through my remarks about what characteristics constitute a successful business professional at MICG.

I wanted people representing MICG to have a particular professional presentation. New employees would learn about "Dress for Success." The financial services profession was a serious business with serious consequences for our clients. I wanted to ensure that our teammates presented themselves professionally. That meant men in well-fitting suits, ties, polished shoes. Women in suits or skirts with proper accessories. I wanted MICG teammates to be instantly recognizable for the care they put into their appearance. This created a synapse-neuron connection with our clients and prospects, which told them we were the correct firm to be handling their financial futures. Prospects and clients would on some level accept that care as evidence that the advisors would put the same care into managing their investments. I wanted MICG team members to stand out in the shipbuilding Virginia town where we were headquartered, and I taught them to dress the same as the CNBC anchors our clients were watching from home.

Since most recruits in our working-class neighborhoods did not reliably possess a professional wardrobe, MICG had a policy of purchasing on behalf of each new team member a wardrobe consisting of three business suits (in blue, black, and gray—earth tones communicated weakness), three shirts/blouses, and three pairs of shoes. Nordstroms outfitted the women; the men were dressed by Beecroft & Bull, a men's fine clothing store in our region. Ashleigh would wear these three suits as a badge of honor for years.

Our orientation focused on communications: not just what we said as representatives of MICG but *how* we said it. This, of course, involved intense phone training. I would circle the office to make sure every time a client said, "thank you," we responded with, "my pleasure." Any violators had to keep a "my pleasure" Post-it note stuck to their computer screen for a week. We called the Ritz Carlton and the Four Seasons hotels—leaders in providing legendary customer service—to inquire about vacations and business services. The goal was to allow MICG team members to learn from the best on how to properly address customers with respect and purpose.

I wanted MICG team members to be the *smartest ones in the room*. All new hires were given a mandatory reading list that included book reports submitted back to me. You can only imagine the look on fifty-year-old successful financial advisors recruited from Merrill Lynch and other big name wire houses when I told them they have to not only read the books but give me a book report. The most important book on the reading list was Dale Carnegie's *How to Win Friends and Influence People*. Our teammates began to understand all business came down to human fundamentals: listening more than speaking, remembering people's names, showing interest in others instead of yourself, and so many more classics we instilled in our everyday actions.

The reading list went on to include *Walk Faster Than Everyone Else*, *How to Enter a Room and Greet Everyone*, *Dining Etiquette*, and a never-ending list of *Investment and Business Core Principles*.

> **Our focus on driving etiquette, character, class, proper human behavior, and superior knowledge created a fundamental base that later, in extreme adversity, positioned me to operate in adverse elements and better navigate the challenges confronting me. I believe with basketball coach Bobby Knight that "Most people have the will to win, few have the will to prepare to win."**

Ashleigh and I had stayed friends even after my nuclear meltdown. After MICG imploded, Ashleigh took a job at Wells Fargo. I took pride in her follow-on success climbing the corporate ladder there. While most of my former colleagues at MICG saw it in their interests to keep their distance from me, Ashleigh never stopped supporting me and letting me know she would always be in my corner. She attended my trial when her busy schedule would allow, and her encouragement meant the world to me.

And then she sent me a love letter. It came to me nearly a year after I had been incarcerated at FCI Fort Dix. I was at one of my lowest points. Receiving her totally unexpected letter was an early miracle in a long list of miracles that would later unfold. She said her friends had held an intervention to tell her that her constant comparison of all men to me had created an impossible situation for her to date someone and not always be focused on what they could do better. She explained that her friends helped her see that she was actually in love with me, and if she didn't pursue this possibility, she would always regret not telling me.

In somewhat of a strange science experiment, Ashleigh had *drunk the Kool-Aid* like no other, and I, humbly but truly, knew she was in love with the *persona of Jeff*, not necessarily in the truly flawed creature that now sat behind rows of barbed wire fences and that had lost a great deal of his confidence and belief in everything he held true before. She said she knew everything would work out, the truth would come to light, and she would stay with me through everything.

I was in shock. I had always known Ashleigh was beautiful and smart, and I had also respected her tremendously for her resilience to overcome a number of childhood challenges, as well as for her fierce independence and determination to be successful on her own. But I never imagined she would pursue a relationship with a man in my perilous position. Ashleigh said in her letter she would visit me at Fort Dix. And as impeccably true to her word as she always was, in short order Ashleigh was waiting for me in the Fort Dix visiting area. I heard my name echoed over the visitor announcements. It wasn't easy. Geography required her to drive seven hours to visit me, which she did every month for the next six years, overcoming prison room visiting hell, until she picked me up to bring me to *our home*. The universe is a baffling enigma. I cannot explain how this happened, or why it happened, but sometimes I seem to be the luckiest man in its wonder. Soon, I want to tell you some great stories about all this.

> **Even though earlier I described how we are all alone with the responsibility to save ourselves when extreme adversity strikes, there are also times when we cannot let our hearts be so hardened, and our plates of armor to be so impenetrable, that we miss a gift that reminds us we are not alone. All the answers are inside us if we are only quiet enough to listen. Ashleigh is a gift, a miracle, and I have spent each day since receiving that letter determined to honor her and make her life a miracle, also.**

Two-Time Felon

The Appeals Court, two years later, crafted a creative way to reaffirm my conviction and decline to order a new, fair trial. That was the bad news. Two pieces of good news, for all the good it did me, were that the Appeals Court overturned my sentence and removed the Honorable Judge Robert Doumar. During my earlier sentencing, in one last bizarre twist, Judge Doumar, inexplicably, stated repeatedly and incorrectly that the Federal Sentencing Guidelines were "mandatory" and thereby he had no discretion but to sentence me to a lengthy imprisonment for more years than most convicted murderers and rapists receive. Even though the law had clearly been settled that US District Court Judges have discretion to impose a sentence they believed appropriate based on all circumstances, Judge Doumar emphasized his contrary beliefs. The Fourth Circuit Court of Appeals wrote, "The district court opined (1) that the Guidelines were 'no longer advisory,' (2) 'It's all where do you fit [in the Guidelines],' and (3) 'I will follow the Guidelines only because I have to. I find that they're not discretionary, they're mandatory'" [No. 13-4828, Doc. 214].

Everyone, except me of course, knew immediately these statements would guarantee my sentence would be overturned. AUSA Brian Samuels and my attorney James Broccoletti knew the Appeals Court could not uphold the sentence. Why did Judge Doumar say what he did? As I learned more about the proceedings, I constantly wondered, *Did he feel guilty? Was he admitting the whole trial was a setup, an orchestrated ambush and this was how he would make sure it was overturned, or that I could at least receive a greatly reduced sentence?* There is so much about this experience I still, today, cannot understand.

But AUSAs Brian Samuels and Katie Dougherty knew my original indictment was going to get reversed. Unwilling to see that happen, the government got to work on Indictment number two to ensure all their expert work in the first trial did not go to waste. In an adversarial justice system, the object is to prevail.

In the FCI Fort Dix law library, I had been carefully crafting my motions to demand the courts allow me to continue to represent myself, *pro se*. I had seen enough of the inner workings of the system to know my only shot was to handle my resentencing myself. Of course that sounds ridiculous to most readers, but I had convinced myself it was the only way I could have a chance of challenging my conviction.

Shackled in chains, I was transported back to Norfolk, Virginia, and was met immediately off the bus by the new court-appointed counsel, Lawrence "Larry" Woodward of Ruloff, Swain, Haddad, Morecock, Talbert & Woodward, P.C., Virginia Beach, Virginia.

James Broccoletti had previously resigned from my case after my mother paid him $25,000 from her Sears pension savings to craft my appeal. He failed to prepare any paperwork, and he refused to return the $25,000. This recovery remains on my life task list today.

Larry Woodward was holding a new indictment to hand to me as I stepped off the bus. What service! He then took me into one of the courthouse meeting rooms and explained that I had a choice. I could continue to represent myself. But if I dropped my demands to proceed *pro se* and allowed him to be my representation for the resentencing and this strange new indictment, he would be able to get me a bond hearing *today* and I would likely be released for the next three to four months with Ashleigh in order for us to properly prepare for the subsequent proceedings. *After two years at violent FCI Fort Dix, I could be released to Ashleigh for up to four months instead of sitting in Western Tidewater Regional Jail?* Larry Woodward even asked Ashleigh if she could bring clothes to the proceeding—she already had them in her trunk—that I could wear home that day. The desire to be with Ashleigh was so palpable I could no longer resist. I was sold!

In remarkably swift orchestration, I was immediately brought before The Honorable US District Court Judge Raymond Jackson who recorded that I was dropping my *pro se* representation and accepting Larry Woodward as defendant's court-appointed counsel. I was then ushered before Magistrate Judge Robert J. Krask, who looking up from the bench, stated, "I see Mr. Martinovich's sentence has been vacated, so as far as I'm concerned he's a free man!" In disbelief I quickly rose to my feet in victory and turned to share the moment with Ashleigh sitting directly behind me in the courtroom. But not so fast. AUSA Brian Samuels leapt from his chair waving a new indictment and pronounced, "Your Honor, there actually is a new indictment, and we are taking Mr. Martinovich upstairs for a bond hearing right now!"

Quickly, now, I was escorted to another courtroom. What incredible service! Most inmates wait months and years just to get in front of one judge. Today I had the honor of appearing before no fewer than three judges. I now found myself before another Magistrate Judge. My lawyer explained the story and the judge seemed to be going with the outcome Woodward suggested would happen. Then AUSA Samuels served another *surprise*. He displayed a large stack of motions I had submitted over the last two years in an attempt to free myself and explained how I had "no remorse and no regret," that by virtue of advocating for myself I obviously did not respect the laws of the US criminal justice system, and that it would be against the public interest to grant me bond.

In a worthy theatrical performance, the judge appeared to be very surprised by these motions and became very concerned about the safety of the community if this violent hedge fund manager was released on bond to be with Ashleigh and able to work on his own defense. "Bond denied!"

The whirlwind orchestration was over. I had given up the right to defend myself. I was now locked away in the Western Tidewater Regional Jail for the next eight months awaiting resentencing with counsel I could not relieve, awaiting a new trial with counsel I could not fire, and angrier than I had ever been on this journey. I had hardened myself to be cynical and cautious, and I had made it back to the point of, possibly, fixing this debacle, and yet again I was defeated!

When battling entrenched adversaries, we must find a delicate balance between cynicism to protect ourselves and humility and optimism to give us the energy to keep going. As exhausting as it may be, we must keep our radar on high intensity to see around corners or otherwise we will be vulnerable to unseen attacks. As strong leaders, we can reestablish our vulnerability and kindness once the threat has passed.

CHAPTER 9

BE A MASTER OF YOUR BUSINESS

Do you know that doing your best is not good enough?

You have to know what to do. Then do your best.

—W. EDWARDS DEMING

I HAD ALWAYS PRIDED MYSELF on being a master of my business. I did not come from wealthy stock or Ivy League connections, so I knew if I were to outperform my peers in the financial services industry I would have to be smarter, and work harder, than everyone else. I studied. I was determined to qualify for more licenses, accreditations, and certifications than anyone else. I broadened my expertise from financial planning to investment banking to financing and lending to trusts and estates to sophisticated insurance and to hedge funds and alternative investments.

I raised my public profile. I spoke regularly at regional seminars and filled panels at national conferences. And I dutifully studied books about leadership and human nature in order to better understand the levers of success through the achievements and failures of others. While it's true that we learn best from failures, the failures do not necessarily have to be our own.

This *chip on my shoulder* to be smarter than everyone else was likely a key to the overconfidence that I had the leadership skills and experience to navigate these treacherous waters. The reality was, I could not. My blindness prevented me from seeing the deficiencies in my skill set and my arrogance kept me from asking for help. These two traits—overconfidence and arrogance—spell doom for anyone in a leadership position. Combine that with the unfortunate reality that followers often reinforce the narcissism of leaders and you get a recipe for disaster.

> One advantage of going through severe adversity for CEOs and other leaders is the purging of the sycophants who have told them what they wanted to hear and empowered the CEOs' reckless or out-of-touch decision-making. It's not difficult to recognize the flatterers. Look for the followers that laugh loudest at the feeble jokes CEOs tell. CEOs as a rule are really not that funny.

My life kept spiraling down, exposing more and more problems. Following my *first conviction*, I told my lawyer James Broccoletti I wanted him to file an appeal as quickly as possible. His immediate response was, "Are you sure you have the money for an appeal?" I assured him I did have the funds, and to my shame, my mother agreed to raid her retirement account to pay for the appeal. Broccoletti filed notice of appeal.

The response from AUSAs Brian Samuels and Katie Dougherty took the form of a scorched earth counterattack. First, they set to work on a plan to stop me from being able to fund my defense. Second, they began to prepare a backup indictment. This second set of charges made less sense to me than the initial set. The background for this part of the government's case against me is a little technical, so I present the following narrative lifted directly from court records and the official transcript.

Un-indemnification Provisions

It's important to start with the three hedge funds operated by MICG Investment Management. The three hedge funds complemented each other with allocations to private investments designed to offer our clients more diversification. The three funds were the MICG Venture Strategies Fund (private equity), Capital Partners Fund (a fund-of-funds portfolio), and Anchor Strategies Fund (a portfolio of selected fixed-income bonds). Together, the funds worked cooperatively to meet capital requirements for larger investments or to provide liquidity for another fund's short-term opportunity. At the time of the 2008 Financial Crisis, the Capital Partners Fund had significant cash values due to the liquidation of a successful prior investment and had cross-invested positions to the Venture Strategies Fund for current private, non-liquid investments.

MICG's Compliance Department, assisted by outside counsel, supervised the operations of the funds to ensure that everything met all regulatory requirements. Todd Lynn of the law firm of Patten Wornom Hatten and Diamonstein in Newport News, Virginia was MICG's lead business attorney. His firm provided oversight of all the compliance requirements of the three hedge funds including the indemnification provisions that indemnify the operators of the funds. These standard-industry provisions are included in every mutual fund prospectus or hedge fund on Wall Street to make it possible for financial professionals to manage investment funds without the fear of being personally sued by clients unhappy with their investments. When investment houses, such as Fidelity, Vanguard, and every other fund company, receive grievances, lawsuits, and even criminal complaints, the indemnification provisions, funded by errors and omissions insurance and assets of the fund, cover the defense and administration of these procedures, all of which are predictable occurrences in our litigious society.

The government took great umbrage that the MICG funds paid for defense attorney James Broccoletti to represent me and MICG for the defense of what we believed was right. The reality is that 98.5 percent of all cases are quickly settled with plea agreements. The government's narrative to the court was that it would be an outrage against the court and shareholders if I were permitted to use the indemnification process to fund my defense. I noted in response that the way the law works in these cases is the indemnification clauses cover fund managers accused of wrongdoing, but if the manager is eventually convicted of the charges, they would be personally responsible for paying the funds back for the expenses of the failed defense. This is the only possible structure in the investment industry. Otherwise, no professional would ever consent to managing investments for someone else.

> When thrown into extreme adversity, we must, first, understand we don't know what we don't know, and commit to 1) realizing our mistakes, 2) instantly becoming more self-aware and educated about our new problem, and 3) mitigate mistakes as quickly as possible to counter the natural progression toward compounding and escalating complications.

My overly cautious lead attorney, Todd Lynn, had previously incorporated a team of separate law firms to represent MICG. The goal was to ensure the fund management and all transactions were independent and beyond legal or ethical reproach for any forms of conflict of interest or mismanagement. Although establishing this level of legal representation was costly, I had approved the structure to ensure the long-term success of the MICG funds and alternative investment platform.

On the federal record, the structure was explained to the court as the following:

"Mr. Lynn worked closely with Mr. Benjamin Biard, Esquire, of Wilson Elser Moskowitz & Dicker Law Firm in New York to provide enhanced expertise in securities law for operations, errors and omissions, legal claims, indemnification, regulatory, and more. To ensure all MICG funds, entities, and individuals received independent representation and that no conflicts of interest were permitted, Mr. Lynn and Mr. Biard further engaged two more legal firms. Mr. Andrew Shilling, Esquire, of Shilling, Pass & Barlow, Chesapeake, Virginia, was engaged to independently represent the MICG Venture Strategies Fund. Mr. Shilling had been Mr. Lynn's roommate at the University of Richmond Law School. Ms. Katherine Klocke, Esquire, of the law firm Akerman, Florida was engaged to independently represent the MICG Partners Fund. Mr. E.D. David, of Law Firm David Kamp & Frank, Newport News, Virginia, provided representation for MICG Anchor Strategies Fund at this time. Mr. Lynn coordinated and orchestrated most procedures among these law firms and was the primary contact for Martinovich."
[Case 4-15-cr-50, Doc. 50, 01/13/17]

These provisions were invoked to pay James Broccoletti and his experts providing the *inconvenient* defense. Mr. Andrew Shilling, esq., was engaged to represent the Venture Strategies Fund, analyze the indemnification provisions, and write an opinion letter confirming everything was being handled properly. He did that. Todd Lynn spoke with James Broccoletti on numerous occasions, and I followed everyone's instructions—until it all imploded, again. On the federal record, the events were explained as follows:

> "Mr. James O. Broccoletti, trial defense counsel, called Martinovich prior to sentencing to let him know there was a problem with the indemnification payments for Broccoletti's fees. The federal agents had visited Mr. Andrew Shilling, the attorney representing MICG Venture Strategies Fund, and Mr. Shilling had for unknown reasons told the agents that he wasn't aware of exactly how the legal fees were paid, or how the proper documentation was executed.
>
> Martinovich drove straight to Mr. Todd Lynn's office, MICG's lead business attorney at Patten Wornom Hatten & Diamonstein (PWHD). After Martinovich relayed the message, Mr. Lynn led Martinovich to PWHD's large conference room and phoned Mr. Shilling, using his cellular instead of the office phone system.
>
> Mr. Lynn questioned Mr. Shilling about the encounter, then became agitated and asked him why he hadn't just told the agents the truth, that all the documentation and authorizations were in place. He continued, 'Of course, you knew the arrangement. That's the whole reason you were hired!' Mr. Lynn ended the call, looked at Martinovich across the con-

ference table and said, 'He's lying. He's scared. He misspoke talking to The Feds and now he's scared to change his story!'

Martinovich responded with a great number of expletives to be translated as, 'What more could go wrong now?!' Mr. Lynn stated that he would follow up with Mr. Shilling and fix the error." [Case 4-15-cr-50, Doc. 50, 01/13/17]

Wells Fargo Fraud Department

After I was accused of masterfully manipulating and defrauding my entire management team, external valuation expert, and independent auditors in my first case, the government now filed a *backup indictment* alleging another "Scheme and Artifice." Under the government's theory of the case, I was accused of defrauding six separate law firms by manipulating their attorneys to fraudulently construct a web of protection for our company, our funds, and shareholders. The government alleged that I "concealed (my) conversion of the investor funds by purporting to have obtained prior authorization for the use of the funds for (my) own personal use and benefit" [Superseding Indictment, 4:15-cr-50, Doc. 10, 02/10/16].

To attempt to drive home this second allegation, "The Scheme and Artifice," AUSAs Samuels and Dougherty scheduled another hearing to present the court with testimony from the director of the Wells Fargo Fraud Department. This executive would explain how I, and my staff, had taken hundreds of thousands of dollars in *cash* withdrawals from the hedge fund bank accounts. Beyond what I believed to be the absurdity of me manipulating all these international law firms, this one *blew my mind* beyond all else. The director of the Wells Fargo Fraud Department described the corporate check cashing system used by Wells Fargo and claimed there were no paper records of our transactions, so "they must have been cash withdrawals."

I could see Judge Doumar's eyes widen as he leaned forward in his seat far above the rest of us. Even he was shocked at this recent exposure. But, in another small miracle, during the massive storm of our meltdown, my small team had kept every check copy Wells Fargo claimed not to possess. I handed copies of these checks to my lawyer. As I recall, Broccoletti dramatically rose from his chair and, waving the checks above his head, said, "You mean these checks?" He moved to mark the checks as evidence.

It was a welcome moment. The government asked the court to verify the checks. One by one, the details of the checks were presented. Here were the checks paid to the document storage company and the auditors. And most of all, here were the checks to the law firms that the Wells Fargo director testified it had no record of. The judge and the court reporter fell back into their chairs, seemingly deflated. I don't know how we found those checks among the myriad boxes of MICG records filling multiple storage units and document storage companies. It was another intervention by the universe that cannot be explained.

To emphasize one more time, through extreme adversity become a master of whatever business you must handle. Never, ever, ever rely on attorneys, accountants, or bankers to do the work you should be doing yourself. They must preserve their own existence and will only go so far in uncovering your truths or standing up for your rights. You must control your destiny.

Sealed

Regardless of the defense's minor victory with the checks, the government followed through and filed the Superseding Indictment. Yet I was unaware of the new danger because it was sealed while I was sentenced for the first indictment and imprisoned in FCI Fort Dix, New Jersey. The government waited to see if the second allegations would be necessary to keep me locked away. But I have one more story about this indictment, which the records states, "was illegally sealed, illegally re-sealed as presented before four Magistrate Judges after having expired, and that included Count One which expired past the applicable statute of limitations" [USCA4 Appeal, 4:15cr50, Doc. 9-1, 9/17/2018].

My later research in the prison law library found the government based its July 15, 2015, motion to seal this indictment on the upcoming expiration of the mail fraud count (sending a letter) that it alleged occurred on July 30, 2010, all based on Statute §3282, which has a statute of limitations of five years. First, it should not have been sealed and held as a backup plan because tolling (holding) is only permissible if there is a primary reason for keeping it secret, such as "apprehending dangerous defendants, stopping defendants from fleeing, (or for) protecting cooperating witnesses" [Rule 6(e) (4)]. Second, it expired, and when it expired any tolling expired, and so the statute of limitations most definitely expired. Third, the record shows the attempt to reseal this indictment, and keep it hidden longer while my appeal was being decided, was presented "before Judge Douglas E. Miller, then before Judge Robert J. Krask, then before Judge Lawrence R. Leonard, and then finally…resealed with a signature by Judge Douglas E. Miller" [Doc. 9-1].

Once I put all this on the record with my *pro se* defense, the new replacement District Court judge, the Honorable Wanda Allen Wright, chose *post hoc* (after the event) to change the actual federal statute used by the government to seal the indictment to a "separate code of statute of limitations, §3293," which holds a ten-year statute of limitations. I couldn't understand how, in this great country of separation of powers, the Judicial Branch could change the Executive Branch's submission.

> Extreme adversity brings what seems like a never-ending flow of crisis after crisis, each with seemingly more intense ramifications. Compartmentalization, the ability to shift *this list* of traumatic problems to one side and use the other side of the brain to refocus on the new dramas right in front of us, is a critical skill for survival.

The Deal

I sat in the Western Tidewater Regional Jail, the same facility the FBI dropped me in back at the beginning of this horrific journey. My court-appointed appeal counsel Larry Woodward visited me more than most inmates. Many inmates only met their court-appointed attorneys minutes before entering their plea deals. While Woodward seemed conscientious, I always believed he had been given clear orders to micromanage and control the defendant (me), whom AUSA Brian Samuels repeatedly referred to as "an economic danger." Like most court-appointed lawyers, he had many clients to serve and the most expeditious way to do that was to get each one to take a plea deal. The last thing most court-appointed lawyers want is to go to trial. Larry and I had numerous screaming matches while I was chained to the desk in the attorney–client meeting room. He demanded I take a plea. I argued that I go to trial, again!

Becoming a little brighter along the way, I took copious notes during each session, mailed the notes to Ashleigh with the stamps she bought me in WTRJ, and she then scanned them and sent them to Woodward and his assistant by email weekly. When everything went south—again—this documentation came in handy in saving my life—again.

I refused to discuss a plea offer for the second indictment. I kept yelling, "This is more ludicrous than the first indictment!" I had come that far standing on what I believed was honorable and principled. I couldn't fold now. My obstinance caused me to sit in the horrific local jail for another eight months before I began to believe the advice, again. Since these experiences I have studied prisoner-captor behavior and negotiations, and I apply it regularly with my consulting clients facing significant transactions and negotiations. I should have studied this earlier.

Being that we had two separate judges, Judge Jackson for the resentencing and Judge Wright Allen for the new indictment, Larry Woodward convinced me he could move both cases to be heard by Judge Wright Allen, and since they had history together she would likely provide more favorable rulings. I became convinced that if I only stopped fighting, the sentence of twelve years would be cut in half, and I could go home now. Ground Five of the submitted Motion pursuant to 28 U.S.C. #2255 stated, "Woodward…convince(d) Martinovich that counsel had negotiated an arrangement with the government and the District Court for Martinovich to receive no more than an aggregate '5-6 years' sentence in return for Martinovich stopping his numerous appeals and 'putting an end to this.' [See Original Memorandum (Doc. 74, Gr. 5), Amended Memorandum (Doc. 89 Gr. 5), amended Martinovich Affidavit #'s 49-78, 102, 104-105, 107-109, and 230-238 (Doc. 90), and Exhibits #1-43]" [No. 18-7061, Doc. 9-1].

Even before the black swan knocks on our doors, we must, sadly, document everything possible to include paperwork, audio recordings, and even video interviews. It saved my life, over and over, during this horrific decade, but I should have implemented this extreme practice twenty years earlier. Today, my consulting associates chuckle when I demand that every contract or disclaimer signing be videotaped.

The night before the joint resentencing, I called Ashleigh on the jail's recorded line. I told her, "The one thing I'm worried about is only you, me, Larry [Woodward], and Judge Allen know about the agreement to come home now in return for dropping all appeals and lawsuits I've filed." I finally told her, and we've discussed it many times since, "At some point in this nightmare, I have to again trust someone, or I will never make it back to you, Cole, and Mom." This phone call was both prophetic and, unfortunately, another teaching lesson I have invoked numerous times since this day.

The next day, hands cuffed and legs shackled, I entered the Walter E. Hoffman United States Courthouse, Norfolk, Virginia, to see a packed courtroom of media, detractors, and, remarkably, a crowd of previous clients, Air Force Academy alumni from around the country, family, and so many friends sitting *on my side*. I couldn't help crying at the overwhelming support, all orchestrated by Ashleigh. I hoped the proceedings would allow me to be released that afternoon so I could enjoy an incredible evening with everyone.

Then Larry Woodward leaned over to me at the table and said, "Hey, I just want to let you know I have to run out of here immediately after this sentencing to another engagement so don't perceive anything negative, or positive, from that. Okay?"

Judge Allen walked into the courtroom with scorn and what I perceived to be a black aura I could feel across the courtroom. Dread came over me instantly. In rushing torments, fear took over my body. The judge began with great purpose. With respect to Ground One of the above-noted court documentation, the judge asserted for the record:

1. "It's something wrong with his brain" [Tr. p.92].

2. "There's something wrong, and I don't know what's wrong" [Tr. p.92].

3. "But there's something wrong, and we're going to get you mental health treatment under my case, because there's something wrong, and it's not been fixed" [Tr. p.92].

4. "It's breaking my heart not to be able to figure out what's wrong" [Tr. p.92].

5. "(I)t's not been fixed" [Tr. p.92].

6. "I know you're not polluting your brain with poison" [Tr. p.92].

7. "There's something wrong. I'm not a doctor, we're going to get mental health treatment, but there's something wrong" [Tr. p.102].

8. "So I don't know what's wrong. I don't. It's complex and sophisticated" [Tr. p.102].

9. "And I'm hoping you get some help to fix that, because you've got a very deep problem" [Tr. p.102].

10. "I'm going to recommend mental health treatment as well" [Tr. p.106].

I was toast. Again. My own fault. Again. I would later submit motion after motion citing legal precedent that if I had such a deep and complex mental health defect how could I have competently entered into any legal contract to allow this next ambush? But to no response of course. The first sentence of twelve years was reinstated. Judge Allen rejected the second case plea agreement that required that sentence run concurrently with whatever reduced sentence was implemented for the first case. Judge Allen, instead, added two more years to my first sentence. I had reversed my sentence for Case One only to receive *more time* than I had started with!

And true to his word, Larry Woodward nearly sprinted out of the courtroom. Ashleigh's later sworn affidavit recounts her story of how she ran after Woodward. She stopped at the top of the courthouse's staircase while Woodward was already at the bottom. She yelled, "Larry what the hell happened?!" He yelled back, "He's lucky he didn't get twenty!" and walked out the courthouse front doors.

JOY TALLEY, TRUE ANGEL

AMIDST MY MELTDOWN, my friends insisted I visit Joy Talley, a highly perceptive *medium* who lived in Virginia Beach, Virginia. Joy spent her life helping others find their paths, understand their possibilities, and create peace amidst the chaos of regular life. She recently left our world for her next adventure, and even though we knew her for a short period, and only spent time with her on a few occasions, Ashleigh and I regularly talk of how much we miss her.

I signed up for an appointment as "JM," wore my post-meltdown uniform of jeans and black cashmere sweater, and walked into the converted tiny home close to the ocean. I was startled by the glow, literally, around Jean, the seventy-something receptionist who greeted me with a friendliness I could actually feel.

Joy, all 4'11" of her, also seventy-something and vibrant, walked out of her office, held both my hands, and said, "You have lost all of your great confidence. Come back here, sit down, and let's talk." A little startled, I sat in the chair, reminding myself to say very little and not to give her any clues with which to manipulate me. I scanned the room full of pictures of her family and portraits of Jesus. She lit a candle, sat quietly, looked *beyond me*, and then began to tell me the story of my last few years.

She refocused on me. "You forgot to dot your *I*'s and cross your *T*'s. You put your trust in the wrong people and now you are going to pay a dear price."

I struggled to not give her any clues or indications of her direct hits.

She continued, "You will lose everything, declare bankruptcy, and even spend time in jail."

I couldn't help myself. I retorted, "There is no chance I will lose everything. I have always won, eventually! And I, definitely, could never be sent to jail!"

She replied, "I see a coffin on your left shoulder. Has someone in your close family recently passed?

"No."

"I'm sorry to tell you that someone soon will." (My father a few months later was told he had stage IV lung cancer and died at the beginning of my trial.)

I sat quietly as she proceeded to narrate the last few years of my life with stunning accuracy, to include names and relevant dollar amounts, and then described my upcoming trials and confinements. With the few minutes left in my allotted appointment, I stopped her and asked, "You have to tell me how you're doing this. Does someone or something tell you?" She explained calmly, "I listen to Bartholomew. He has guided me my entire life." She continued, "You have been going through difficult times, and you are going to go through much more difficult times, but if you keep your faith in God, you will, eventually, make it through this."

She stood, walked over to me, hugged me, and held my hand as she led me out of her office. In the following months and years, I would have moments of clarity, and almost déjà vu, remembering how Joy had described these events long before.

Before receiving our Appeals Court order, I urged Ashleigh to see Joy for the first time for an update. Joy told Ashleigh I would reverse my case but for some reason not come home yet because "many bad people" behind the scenes were working against us. The accuracy of her insights gave me chills. She told Ashleigh a "public speaker" (her term for a politician) was interfering on behalf of wealthy previous clients to not let the conviction be reversed. Ironically, two separate attorneys would later report to me the same description. She also seemed to warn Ashleigh by repeating, "You do know that Jeff walks *in* the *out* door, and he will never be able to work for someone else." And, "You do know you are in love with him." To the last statement, Ashleigh continued to hold her ground and responded, "Absolutely not!"

Years later, after I made my way down to FCI Beckley Minimum-Security Camp in West Virginia, I became eligible for the CARES Act releases to home confinement during the COVID-19 pandemic. Unfortunately, my name was never called, as I had concluded the rules never applied to me and I battled self-pity daily watching others get transferred home. Ashleigh visited Joy one more time attempting to receive some insight we could leverage. Joy told her, "The same bad people are stopping him from being released." Joy took her outside, asked her to pull up a picture of me on her phone, and laid it in on the sidewalk. Joy poured salt around the phone in a circle and remained quiet. She then stated, "Next Friday they will call Jeff's name. He will be the second on the list." The following Friday, the speaker blared "Martinovich #81091-083 report to counselor Johnson's office." I was the second name called.

Finally, when I was eventually released home, Ashleigh said we had to call Joy and let her know! Joy was aging and would soon pass at age ninety-one, February 18, 2022, onto her next adventure, but our call brought her almost as much *joy* as we were experiencing, ourselves. Before I hung up, she said, "You will be moving soon and your two children are going to thrive."

I reminded her that I only had one child, Cole. She corrected me, "No, you have two, the other one just hasn't arrived, yet."

I protested, "I'm 55 years old. I don't think that's going to happen!"

She provided her last words of wisdom. "Don't worry. You're going to do great!"

We soon, unexpectedly, moved to a beautiful new home in downtown Ghent, Norfolk, Virginia, and Ashleigh delivered my second child Carleigh, shortly thereafter, just as Joy prophesized. We all miss her dearly.

CHAPTER 10

SHIFT YOUR PERSPECTIVE

When you change the way you look at things,
the things you look at change.

—DR. WAYNE DYER

MY GOAL IN ALL MY ADVISORY BUSINESSES was to genuinely improve the financial lives of the people I served. I strove to find win–win scenarios, because I've always believed in abundance, versus scarcity. For my colleagues, I sought work environments in which everyone in the organization could achieve their own desired objectives. But it wasn't entirely altruistic. I had my eyes on my own interests. Still, I had learned, early on, that helping others achieve would in turn reward me tenfold. This was my philosophy of personal success.

Now, imprisoned as I was, I realized that this set of perspectives was not enough to protect me in my current environment. After being locked up for four years, I realized I needed a new set of perspectives. Circumstances called for me to adopt a completely new paradigm in order to survive the adversity I was facing.

Some people believe because you come in peace you aren't prepared for war. I needed to now show that I had the strength to wage a war for my survival as well as the truth. I believed I had followed all the proper steps. I had patiently exposed the injustice and inaccuracies. I patiently allowed the system to correct. But it was like spitting into the wind. None of my efforts showed results. I didn't know what to do. Maybe I had to redouble my efforts? Maybe, I realized, my perspective—that the extreme adversity I was facing could be addressed by strong and persistent effort—was no longer rational.

I faced the possibility that a new perspective was in order. Maybe win–win scenarios don't work in prison. I saw I would have to adopt a zero-sum perspective and implement a scorched earth, take-no-prisoners strategy, the strategy AUSA Brian Samuels practiced so effectively on me.

I changed my whole approach to dealing with adversity. And for that, I had to shift my perspective. Here's the thing. I thought I was pretty good at thriving on change. But like most CEOs, I was only pretty good at adapting to changes I chose or could control. What is adversity but unwelcome change?

I needed to learn how to harness change that blindsided me and transform it into a force for growth instead of destruction. As I headed into what looked like years of incarceration, I needed to strengthen my relationship to change. A shift in perspective is what the situation required.

> **When you confront conditions you neither chose nor can readily manage, it is helpful to shift your perspective. That shift can take many forms. But the common element is by thinking or doing something differently to change yourself or your situation. Shifting one's perspective expands the imagination, increases focus, and streamlines the main goal of leaders: to find clarity.**

It's never easy to shift one's perspective. It's even more difficult for successful and powerful people. As I mentioned earlier in the book, a CEO never tells a great joke but that everyone always laughs. As a CEO, I knew two things with certainty. I was never going to get handed a cold cup of coffee and I was never going to hear the whole truth. Moreover the personal paradigms that led to my success were rarely challenged. As a consequence, I had little or no incentive to change my views and adopt others. But all perspectives have a limited shelf life. The world is changing too fast for even the most effective viewpoints to remain fixed.

I had the additional problem of being incarcerated. The more limited your options, the more difficult it is to change one's perspective. After all, one of the conventional strategies for adopting a new panorama is to reframe a situation from "I Have To" into "I Get To." Well, in prison there are hundreds of "I Have To's" and almost zero "I Get To's." Still, I found some.

Changing the words we use has the power to reveal agency we didn't know we had. When greeted by a fellow inmate with, "How ya doing?," I would respond with a chuckle and a hearty "Fabulous!" Or "Fantastic!" They may have been laughing at what they considered my naivety. What they missed is that reality is constructed by how we see the world. For example, when I spoke about my goals, I would always express them in *done terms* or *acting as if.* Sometimes it's called fake it till you make it. By whatever term, the practice contradicts hopelessness, activates agency, and increases the odds that I will actually accomplish my goals. So I would say things like, "After the Fourth Circuit reverses my case, we are going to have one incredible party at the Bistro!" "Right after I rebuild MICG #2 and restore our team, *60 Minutes* is going to love that story!" I constantly reminded myself that speaking success into existence, even when appearing nearly impossible, had worked over and over for me in my life.

> Organizational hierarchies prevent leaders from getting essential truths and candid opinions, especially if they contradict opinions contrary to what followers think the leader wants to hear. We struggle because we get told only a portion of what we need to know. We have to demand, "Look, I need to hear what I'm missing. Tell me what you're not telling me." And then we must listen and, most importantly, never punish or ostracize bearers of bad news.

Change Something, Anything

Another way I shifted my perspective was to just change something. Anything. It hardly matters. Simply doing something differently allows our minds to open to other possibilities. Eventually, we can move on to changing bigger things that more directly impact the adversity we need to manage.

Still another way I shifted my perspective was to react in radical, unusual ways. When conditions change, there's little profit in doing the same things in response to the same problems. It had never been my strategy, or my style, and I wasn't even sure I had enough negative energy (*or was it positive?*) to continue to wage this battle, but it was my only hope to save my life, get back to my family, and finally make right the pain my mistakes had caused for so many people. Fourteen years on a metal bunk would just guarantee defeat for everyone!

As soon as I arrived back at FCI Fort Dix, after weeks of traveling cuffed and shackled through multiple county jails, with stories that would make your toes curl, I tripled my efforts to help other inmates make progress in their own cases. This intense directed energy to help their station in life gave me tremendous positive energy back into my life.

> Here's a truth demonstrated repeatedly through history: when people experience extreme adversity but focus on helping others instead of themselves, the human spirit is energized and begins to heal itself. Serving others is a gift that rebounds to the gift-giver. The practice represents the most potent medicine to avoid despair and self-pity while regaining one's own strength and self-confidence.

I would periodically lose my temper and rage against inmates who had given up, or even more so against those who mindlessly repeated their court attorneys' mantra, "You better not upset the judge!" The inmates quickly tired of me quoting from the 2015 movie *Bridge of Spies*. It was one of the movies I got to watch stealthily in the prison chapel thanks to the unauthorized import business of our inmate chapel clerk, AJ. The movie inspired me.

Briefly, convicted Russian spy Rudolf Abel tells the following story to his lawyer (played by Tom Hanks): "This one time, I was at the age of your son, our house was overrun by partisan border guards. Dozens of them. My father was beaten, my mother was beaten, and this man, my father's friend, he was beaten. And I watched this man. Every time they hit him, he stood back up again. So they hit him harder. Still he got back to his feet. I think because of this they stopped the beating.

They let him live. '*Stoikiy muzhik*' I remember them saying. Which sort of means like uh, 'standing man' . . . 'standing man.'"

I've had a lot of time to think about the movie and the Russian term "stoikiy muzhik." Although the movie translates the term to mean "standing man," my research suggests a better translation is "resilient man" or "tough man." And the takeaway is that inmates who stand their ground in the face of adversity will certainly get abused but if they retain hope and dignity, they will often command some level of grudging respect from their abusers.

It was clear to me that inmates who stood up for themselves actually received better treatment from the guards, counselors, and the courts. On the other hand, I saw precious few inmates advocating for their rights. It was much easier to give up and go along to get along. This mindset drove me crazy, because prison life was the only environment I had ever experienced where the more you appeased the powers that be, the more you were exploited and degraded. Complicity and cooperation in this bizarre system only brought people less nutrition, fewer opportunities for recreation, more restriction of movement, and, bizarrely, more contempt from the courts.

We achieved a few small victories that shortened sentences or received a favorable ruling. We celebrated every time such a decision allowed an inmate to *get back into court* after long giving up hope of any positive resolution. Their hope gave me hope.

Perspective is limitless; it cannot be confined. Even in prison there are ways to shift your perspective. One way that worked for me was to reset my endgame. While the goals of reversing my sentence, getting out of prison, and, later, reuniting with Ashleigh remained the overarching objectives, it helped me reset my goals to something that I might—might!—be able to possibly achieve. For example, I reset my endgame to set myself up in a better position to go after my ultimate goals. For me that meant the next step, for now, was to get my ass transferred from FCI Fort Dix to a less restrictive work camp.

Martinovich v. Ortiz, Warden, FCI Fort Dix

I reset my endgame to persuade the Bureau of Prisons to transfer me to a minimum-security facility camp generally housing nonviolent inmates convicted of white-collar offenses such as insider trading or tax evasion. To have even the remotest possibility of challenging my conviction, I needed an environment where my physical security was not in question every day. Surviving at FCI Fort Dix was a full-time job. Despite my best efforts to keep my head down, I collected two *physical* scars to show for my incarceration, unfortunately with no great heroic stories. And I knew that if I didn't get out, the mental toll of just staying alive would crowd out any opportunity to work on my case. If I could manage to get transferred to a prison camp, I would have better opportunities for programs and resources that just might allow me to make it home sooner.

For four years I had failed repeatedly with the Bureau of Prison's Administrative Remedy program to achieve this transfer. I continually filed grievance after grievance in their system: Form BP-8 to the counselor. Denied. Form BP-9 to the Warden. Denied. Form BP-10 to the Regional Office. Denied. Form BP-11 to the Washington D.C. Headquarters. Denied. Not to be deterred, I would begin again. Sometimes, the denial would not even make it back to me before the time allotted to be able to file the next appeal up the chain, so I would be administratively disqualified. In that case, I needed to start the entire process again. This cycle achieved zero results for four years.

Then one day, I received a Freedom of Information Act (FOIA) package at mail call.

FOIA is the system put in place to grant US citizens access to public documents and information, as a reminder that the government is actually organized for *We the People* and its purpose is to serve the people. In addition to filing hundreds of court motions and petitions, I had also filed a number of FOIA requests seeking any information possible with which I could understand the charges against me, as well as the proceedings and the reasons for the continuous failure of my efforts. I wrote to the FBI, IRS, Treasury Department, Bureau of Prisons, and numerous Department of Justice administrative divisions, to include the Inspector General. They would deny my requests, or claim I had to pay them thousands of dollars for copying expenses. Of course, I had no way of paying large sums for copying costs. I would simply redouble my efforts and send more requests, more letters, more appeals.

To my astonishment, this new package contained multiple answers to my requests for copies of communications between FCI Fort Dix and the office of the Norfolk, Virginia, US attorney. I had sought information on why I was being held at a higher security prison against the BOP's own policies. The pages all had "FOIA EXEMPT" boldly stamped at the bottom, the nomenclature I came to learn meant do not release for FOIA requests. According to the Secret Service, the exemptions "protect against the disclosure of information that would harm: national security, the privacy of individuals, the proprietary interests of business, the functioning of the government, and other important recognized interests."

I wondered why my placement at FCI Fort Dix would be exempt, and how did these documents end up in the package sent to me. Was it a clerical mistake, or did the universe intervene again and nudge a government clerk to forward the pages despite the markings on the documents?

The memorandum and email copies stated, "Mr. 'redacted' indicated that he cannot recommend the inmate to a camp but the (sic) is up to the Bureau of Prisons." In bold it continued, "He also indicated not to reveal to the inmate about the pending cases."

Finally it concluded, "(B)ased on the email from the AUSA about outstanding/unresolved charges in his first case, request a MGTV to keep inside the fence." An MGTV was a Management Variable for Greater Security assigned to an inmate if keeping him at a higher security prison instead of placing him at the safer, minimum-security facility his charges and current length of sentence dictate.

Given that I finally *exhausted all administrative remedies*, four years later, I was legally permitted to file for resolution in the federal courts. In the US District Court of New Jersey I filed *Martinovich v. Ortiz, Warden, FCI Fort Dix*, explaining I had been wrongfully kept at a higher security institution for all these years with my large stack of submissions for transfers summarily denied. Remarkably, within days, after four years, FCI Fort Dix's legal department submitted a response motion to the courts claiming this issue was *moot* and should be dismissed because "he is currently awaiting re-designation to a minimum-security prison camp, and the transfer will likely occur within the next few weeks" [submitted by Craig Carpenito, US Attorney, March 15, 2018]. How ironic. The courts and the BOP, of course, never want to have a consequential decision that could be used as precedent by other inmates.

True to their word, I was shortly transferred to FCI Beckley, West Virginia, a minimum-security camp with no fence and two hundred, instead of four thousand, inmates. I took the job as the new head law library clerk and resumed my mission to make my way back home.

Martinovich v. Lefsih

By searching my own name in the law library computers, an act that always brought me despair reliving each proceeding, I discovered *United States v. Hemza Menade Lefsih*, a Fourth Circuit Court of Appeals case. Lefsih was an Algerian immigrant taxi driver whose appeal not only contained the exact same variables as mine, to include an unruly judge and a defense attorney who never once objected and preserved the violations, but the same Fourth Circuit Appeals Court overturned Lefsih's conviction and ordered a new, fair trial, by referencing *my* personal case as precedent thirteen times in the Published Opinion and Order!

I hurried to prepare and submit a Motion to Recall the Mandate Pursuant to 28 U.S.C. #1651 All Writs Act based on this obvious contradiction. Even though nearly all recall the mandate motions are denied immediately, I was heartened, and even allowed myself to become optimistic, that the Fourth Circuit ordered the government to file a Response to my submission. The doctrine of Horizontal Stare Decisis mandates a court, especially an Appeals Court, must adhere to its own prior decisions, unless it finds compelling reasons to overrule itself [Black's Law, 9th Ed.].

I had laid out a clear and objective comparison of the exact same variables with which the court denied my new trial and, contrarily, granted Lefsih's. It was black and white. AUSA Brian Samuels and USA Dana J. Boente submitted a seventeen-page response, which I always termed *rinse and repeat*, that instead of addressing the legal arguments repeated page after page of what a terrible, evil person I was and, most importantly, that I had never expressed *regret and remorse*. I would always rage about how the subjective issues seemed to carry the day and overwhelmed logical arguments supported by evidence and facts.

In fact, I had consistently expressed deep regret for my long list of leadership failures which resulted in damage to so many people who deserved better. More importantly, I had repeatedly vowed to remedy my errors of judgment. This vow I take seriously. My goal is to do all in my power to make whole all those hurt by my leadership failures. The problem remained that I refused to express remorse and regret for the underlying allegations against me. I believed then as I do now that the accused should be able to defend their positions without being penalized for advocating for themselves.

Despite my best efforts at crafting the legal argument, the Fourth Circuit denied the motion [*United States v. Martinovich, 810 F.3d 232, 238 (4th Cir. 2016)*; *United States v. Lefsih, No. 16-4345*].

When facing great adversity, the high-profile leader must understand that public opinion and *system opinion* will likely be entrenched against them. Leaders must realize their efforts, arguments, remedies, and solutions must be far beyond what they would previously have found proportionate and equitable. Leaders must accept, and commit to, giving outsized efforts many times greater than everyone else in order to achieve a survivable, or, better yet, victorious, solution.

Ineffective Counsel

Once all your motions, petitions, appeals, and US Supreme Court filings have been denied, as nearly five hundred of mine had been, the last path available to an inmate is to make, basically, the same arguments rephrased in the manner *it was my attorney's fault!* This Statute 28 U.S.C. # 2255 provides a path back into court for Ineffective Assistance of Counsel. If your attorney provided such a demonstrably terrible representation in your case, you could, possibly, have the opportunity to submit your issues before the court, again. As with everything else, the tremendous majority of these submissions are denied, but I believed that if anyone had a strong case for this, I had to have a chance here.

Since I was now officially a *two-time felon*, the term the government would repeatedly submit to reinforce its position, I was now, in the government's eyes, an even more horrible excuse for a human being and would need to tender two separate submissions. The first submission focused on ineffective representation by my trial lawyer, James Broccoletti. The second focused on the ineffective representation provided by my court-appointed attorney Larry Woodward, with respect to the debacle that was my resentencing hearing.

It was now 2017. In regard to my trial, I naively believed I had a decent chance to get some relief since the Appeals Court had already presented a rare rebuke of a US District Court Judge and the clear explanation of how the reversal could not occur due to the ineffectiveness of James Broccoletti to never once object to the bizarre trial. With the second case, I had fortunately been super diligent in documenting all the legal strategy and negotiations that went into my accepting the joint agreement to put these cases behind me. As I recounted, overzealous prosecutors hijacked the proceedings. Representations made to me were violated. Larry Woodward literally ran out the back of the courtroom leaving me to serve more time than the original sentence I had appealed. Not only did I fail in my desire to get home, but the net-net was an addition of two extra years to my original sentence. Thank you for playing!

I submitted my petitions to the Honorable Judge Wanda Wright Allen of the Eastern District of Virginia, the presiding judge for both cases now that the sentences had been combined and increased. She would not respond for an *entire year*. I filed a Writ of Mandamus to the Fourth Circuit Court of Appeals to compel her to at least respond. Nothing. I filed another Writ of Mandamus, and the Fourth Circuit Court of Appeals finally compelled her to, at least, respond.

The Honorable Wanda Allen Wright dismissed as having zero merit every single ground, eighteen in all, among the two cases. The responses in many instances seemed totally irrelevant to the argument made. I didn't know if these were her writings or responses from one of the clerks just out of law school that routinely handle the workload of federal district judges.

It was now 2018. I submitted the appeals, again, to the Fourth Circuit Court of Appeals. To my astonishment, the Appeals Court reversed Judge Allen's decisions on five separate grounds, again practically unheard-of results. I remember the day I received notices of the reversals. Mike, my fantastic cellmate at Beckley West Virginia, and I sat there reading in disbelief the orders that finally—finally!—went my way.

When you're cellmates, the setbacks of one become the setbacks of the other. Though incredibly rare, good news such as what I received is shared with cellmates. Mike had suffered with me through the depression and temper tantrums that followed the hundreds of denials I received over the years. At first, neither of us dared believe

I was actually making progress. Here it was in black and white: The Fourth Circuit determined for the sake of justice numerous issues had to be addressed from my trial as well as the debacle of my resentencing hearing. As a result, I was entitled to an Evidentiary Hearing in Norfolk, Virginia. It was to be me, *pro se* (that is, representing myself) now pitted against my former attorneys, Broccoletti, esquire and Larry Woodward, esquire, as well as my old nemesis, AUSA Brian Samuels.

A Fool for a Client

It is said that any defendant who represents himself has a fool for a client. There's truth in the matter. I was a fool. Nevertheless, painful experience demonstrated that relying on lawyers was even more foolish. I had my work cut out for me.

I then requested the Honorable Judge Wanda Wright Allen recuse herself. My motion argued that it was proper for her to recuse herself given her intemperate handling of my resentencing hearing and her cursory, summary dismissals of my injustices, now validated. Judge Allen refused to recuse herself. I persisted. The Appeals Court ordered her to rule on her own recusal. She refused again. I wrote to the new Chief Judge of the Eastern District Virginia highlighting her clear conflicts of interest and questionable behavior noted by the Court of Appeals.

My escalating the matter apparently worked. Judge Wanda Wright Allen recused herself from my case. It was the second time a judge passing judgment over me was removed.

It was May 19, 2020. I was on my way home, again, for hearings to, hopefully, put an end to this horrific journey seven years early, and seven years too late.

> In extreme adversity, the waterfall seems to gain more force and velocity against you in a never-ending current. Then one day, sometimes imperceptibly, the tide starts to turn. Getting to the camp, winning a couple reversals, removing the latest impediment to justice. And then you gain momentum, compound your victories, begin to turn the tide of power, and even begin to take control of the narrative. Joel Osteen said, "We don't have to win, sometimes we just have to outlast them."

But even a glimpse of victory left a bitter taste.

To overcome adversity, above all else, it's critical for leaders to face tomorrow and move forward. Almost any movement will do. It's rare for leaders dealing with adversity to see the ultimate destination, but we must. As I recounted in chapter 3, I had to focus my gaze inexorably forward. As Rabbi Kalman Packouz said, "You can live in the past, but there's no future in it."

I craved a different future so badly I could taste it.

CHAPTER 11

WATCH FOR THE TURNING TIDE

There is something good in all seeming failures.
You are not to see that now. Time will reveal it. Be patient.

—SIVANANDA SARASWATI

AMIDST ALL MY SETBACKS, I did manage one victory.

With my transfer to FCI Beckley, a minimum-security facility for male inmates in West Virginia, I now had more opportunities to improve myself by helping others as I helped myself. I was assigned to the adjacent satellite camp, the least restrictive facilities in the federal prison system. Picture army barracks with half-walls separating you and you're your *cellie* from everyone else, a relatively low staff-to-inmate ratio, and no perimeter fencing. Although a few of my fellow inmates were convicted of white-collar offenses, the vast majority were guilty of nonviolent drug offenses. All residents, like me, had less than ten years to serve on their sentences.

One of the best parts of now being housed in a prison camp is that it offered more freedom of movement. I got permission to create a business course. Easier said than done. I struggled in vain to find any actual curriculum or outlines of training programs for the rehabilitation and preparation of these inmates who would soon be reentering the real world. So I had to create them.

I thought back on how my professors had organized their courses. I remembered the dozens of training seminars and leadership programs I had attended. The best ones had a particular structure that parceled out the information in manageable chunks, as well as using humor and storytelling to make the lessons engaging. I would definitely have to soften my anger and work to find some long-lost jokes and banter.

My goal in presenting a business course was twofold. First, I was sincerely interested in being of service and giving back some of the good fortune I had been graced with in the early part of my career. Second, I knew that the best way to master the concepts necessary for me to take control of the second chapter of my own life would be to teach them.

Building Special Communities

The result was a twenty-five-week course titled *Building Special Companies*. The goal was to introduce basic elements of entrepreneurship, including concepts of business structure, financing, hiring, talent management, and leadership. It was an opportunity for me to share the secrets and strategies that enabled me to build MICG Investment Management into a billion-dollar company before it all came crashing down. The inmates who completed *Building Special Companies* especially enjoyed the stories of the innumerable business mistakes I made along the way. That laughter made the course not only enjoyable but effective.

I was humbled by the strong attendance and participation the course generated. It was clear there was a hunger among my fellow inmates for real-world lessons from one of their own. Their enthusiasm was contagious. Some of the attendees also had great business experiences, and I learned as much from them as they learned from me. Organizing and teaching the course over the years pushed me to understand my business successes and failures in a more coherent way. I look forward to publishing many of those lessons in an upcoming book titled *Icarus: From Zero to a Billion to Zero* soon. Stay tuned for details.

I also taught classes on interviewing skills, resume writing, and job search perseverance. My fellow inmates loved it when I asked them to role-play the various scenarios the course touched on. For example, the segment on how to conduct yourself during a job interview with a not-so-friendly new boss was very popular, with all of us laughing at how easy it was for an interview to quickly fall apart.

Resource for Inmates

In the law library, I wrote a great number of compassionate release submissions. Federal law permits sentence reductions and early releases for certain dying, incapacitated, and elderly prisoners. Getting a compassionate release is not easy. The process starts with an inmate, or someone acting on his behalf, making a request in writing to the warden. The Bureau of Prisons recognizes a number of grounds for compassionate release, including age, medical conditions, and family circumstances. Most submissions for compassionate release generally include a release plan detailing where the inmate will live and how his needs, including medical needs, will be met. It was discouraging that every one of these submissions was rejected.

I set myself up in the law library as a resource for other inmates. I helped write and type resumes. I wrote employment cover letters for soon-to-be released inmates. A few inmates were interested in investment strategies and I held informal evening seminars where I would answer their questions about markets and asset classes such as equities, bonds, and commodities. Whenever someone challenged me to explain how it was that I knew so much, I would always answer in the same way: only because I have made more mistakes than anyone!

This positive energy, which I could feel repairing my soul, even gave me the motivation to write another book I had dreamed of writing. When speaking and writing business lessons, I had always made a long list of life lessons which really didn't fit into a business book, but that I believed were so critical to personal success. I had been incredibly fortunate in my life to have so many brilliant mentors: my father, my coaches, and my military and business leaders who took me under their wings. I wanted to convey these great lessons and life theories to all the people never fortunate to have these opportunities. So, with my favorite No. 2 pencil and manual typewriter I was able to create *Just One More: The Wisdom of Bob Vukovich*, which Ash Press would later publish. These projects gave my mind a small break from the intense focus and anger.

> When committed to overcoming extreme adversity, once the tide begins to turn we can, literally, feel momentum building in our favor. Just as a PGA golfer feels his swing suddenly hit the right groove, and week after week he surprises the field with multiple victories, we have to take advantage of this break in the storm. We see sun rays streaming through the storm clouds, and we have to redouble our efforts and begin to change our angle of effort from just merely surviving to, possibly, winning and thriving.

COVID-19: Risk and Opportunity

It was April 2020, and the COVID-19 pandemic was impacting every workplace and institution. Besides patients in hospitals, there are few populations more at risk of sickness and death than those incarcerated. Imprisoned people are infected by the coronavirus at a rate more than five times higher than the nation's overall scale. The inability to quarantine or practice social distancing, together with overcrowding and inadequate medical resources, imperiled the lives of many people incarcerated in jails and prisons.

The pandemic spawned misinformation and disinformation in the real world. In the information vacuum of prison, rumors and misinformation ran rampant, and prison administrators usually respond to crises with lockdowns. In the present crisis, this was probably the worst response. Lockdowns just spread the infection more. In our prison camp, we had more room to move around, yet the warden confined us to our tight quarters, while a significant number of staff and guards suddenly stopped reporting to work.

As the pandemic worsened, Congress offered inmates a window of opportunity. Congress passed the CARES Act, which permitted minimum-security inmates, mostly at camps, to be moved to home confinement to reduce the prison overcrowding during the pandemic. It was not lost on me that the miracle of this opportunity was available to me only because I had fought for over four years to be moved from FCI Fort Dix to this minimum-security camp.

Over 12,000 inmates have seen CARES Act home confinement placements. I was one of them. The conditions of home confinement were still serious, but, again, another marked incremental improvement. I had to wear an ankle monitor people would nickname "the microwave" due to its size and weight. I had a case manager I had to report to. I had to get a job and keep it. And I was required to be available to answer phone calls at random times during the day and night, four to five times a day, every day.

By all accounts, this unplanned program has been a resounding success. One clear goal of the program was to reduce the spread of COVID-19 within the confined space of prisons by decreasing the density of inmate populations. Another was to reduce prison populations without jeopardizing public safety. On that score, the program was a resounding success. Of the 12,000 people released to home confinement under the CARES Act, the Bureau of Prisons reported that only seventeen of them committed new crimes. In the context of a recidivism rate in a country where it's normal for 30–65 percent of people coming home from prison to reoffend within three years of release, we're talking about a recidivism rate of 0.15 percent.

When battling for survival, we must take advantage of every opportunity life presents us, even if the window is only slightly cracked open and it is impossible to connect the dots to an eventual benefit. Just as in business where we must constantly train ourselves to say "yes" to the smallest invitations, which may turn into great successes, in adversity we must fight the natural inclinations of pessimism, hopelessness, and not *swinging at every pitch.* **It was always the motions, the arguments, and the changes which I never thought would make a difference that helped me blindly navigate my way to survival and restoration.**

It helped that my prison disciplinary record was clean as a whistle. Some of this was due to my determination to follow the rules and stay off the *radar screen*. Some of it, I'm convinced, was sheer providence. As a result I had the lowest possible PATTERN assessment, a tool the Bureau of Prisons uses to predict the likelihood of recidivism (having to be returned to prison). PATTERN, announced in July 2019, stands for Prisoner Assessment Tool Targeting Estimated Risk and Needs.

Home Confinement

My name was on the list to go home! My risk profile, based on my age, convictions, education, participation in prison programs, and clean disciplinary record, was the lowest possible. I let everyone know I was on the way home, Ashleigh prepared to come rescue me, and I tried not to lose my mind in anticipation. But with the Bureau of Prisons, nothing comes at face value. I was, then, notified I was off the list to go home! There was confusion with the requirements across the BOP, and now I did not qualify. I told everyone the devastating news and took my place back on my metal bunk. I couldn't believe the despair and disappointment I continually caused my family.

The *Twilight Zone* is about the only way I could describe these flirtations with freedom against the daunting future of seven more years in prison. Also, I knew in my heart that if I could function outside the constraints of prison, have access to the internet and records, I could succeed in the upcoming evidentiary hearings I had been granted by the Fourth Circuit Court of Appeals. I would, finally, correct my case, restore my family and stakeholders, and begin to repair so much damage caused by all my mistakes.

Then Attorney General Bill Barr read the Bureau of Prisons the riot act. On March 26, 2020, the attorney general directed Michael Carvajal, the director of the Bureau of Prisons, to speed up the process of granting qualified inmates home confinement. "Prioritize the use of your various statutory authorities to grant home confinement for inmates seeking transfer in connection with the ongoing COVID-19 pandemic," Barr wrote in his directive. I was back on the list!

Soon it was the long-awaited day. Ashleigh picked me up at the front gate in a scene out of The Blues Brothers movie, where Elwood Blues picks up his brother, Jake, at Joliet Prison. I had left my coffee mug on the ground as we drove off. I was still in confinement mode, and I actually demanded we go back to get it. "Are you insane?" Ashleigh screamed. Little did she know how accurate the question was at the moment.

But I just couldn't leave the coffee mug behind. It was, literally, my only possession in the world, and I could not lightly let it go. It would take some months for me to begin to *deinstitutionalize*. Ashleigh turned around, I picked up my lone possession, and then we were off. Ashleigh best describes those days of me exhibiting a somewhat unbelievable, positive demeanor in the sunlight, as I had trained myself, but by nightfall, my optimism and good cheer would be replaced by nightmares and futile battles with phantom opponents. To be honest, it still is.

> Leaders need to be honest with themselves that great adversity takes a toll on their physical and mental health, as well as the soul, and that repair time will be necessary. Fortunately, great leaders are normally not the types who wallow in this misery but that have great strength and experience to rebound from failure, lick their wounds, and charge forward. We simply need to acknowledge this serious step in the process.

Getting a Grip on Life Again

Miracles kept coming my way. My home confinement day job, offered by a friend of Ashleigh's, allowed me to manage and grow a minority/women-owned small business serving the local shipyard. In the first six months we grew year-over-year sales by over 67 percent, and I couldn't believe my luck. I was back in business, being productive, and making a positive difference. My close friends, most of whom had decided to stick with me, sprang into action. My Air Force Academy roommate, Brian, had done very well for himself. He flew his newly acquired Gulfstream IV private jet from San Diego to sit down with me and provide a long list of companies and projects he needed help with. I clearly remember how happy I was about others' successes when, before this experience, I would have been jealous or competitive. Now, I was only overwhelmed with gratitude for these opportunities.

I rose before dawn to make progress on the new commitments. It felt amazing to be in charge of my own time for the first time in years. I also had to prepare for the upcoming evidentiary hearings, before commuting to my home confinement *day job*. As required, the large ankle monitor I displayed would buzz throughout the day while the GPS tracked my movements. The halfway house would call four to five times per day and night to also confirm my location, as well as bring me in every week for drug testing. With great difficulty, I secured a driver's license and a bank account to deposit my modest weekly paycheck. I intently focused on the positive path to restoration while battling the reality of completely starting over with *Google Factor Shame*. If you googled my name, you would get five pages of results vividly describing my excesses and failures.

Recovery from extreme adversity and failure happens in *fits and spurts*. We must become comfortable living with roadblocks at every turn. Just when we feel we are making progress, the phone will ring, or the summons will appear, and we are back in fight-or-flight mode. We have to stay focused and realize it remains a long journey and not let recurring adversity break our spirit for ultimate recovery.

And one of the most surprising restoration miracles? On New Year's Eve night, 2020, Ashleigh whispered in my ear, "We are pregnant!" I was fifty-six. My son was twenty-seven. And now I was set to start a new family with a baby girl we would name Carleigh. It was just like Joy had prophesized (see page 146). Ashleigh and I were *over the moon*, and I allowed myself to take a breath and thank the universe for saving me and giving us this miracle. I ran up and down the stairs for the exercise and took extra doses of vitamins. I had to stay strong for another twenty years! After we had decided on the name Carleigh, Ashleigh checked the meaning of the name. She started to cry and showed me the phone. It read, "Free Man."

With conflicting emotions, but also great relief, I withdrew all my legal proceedings to overturn my conviction. The costs of appeal were too high. The last time I tried that, my sentence was *increased*. With little Carleigh on the way, I could not risk *winning*, however unlikely, as I had already experienced the backlash of more charges and longer sentences. After seven long years, I now knew I could not risk the results of standing up for what I believed was right. On April 4, 2022, the US District Court for the Eastern District of Virginia accepted my withdrawal and, once and for all, closed my case [Doc. 379].

Restoration

I served many masters while working to rebuild the world. I knew that to restore my employees, my shareholders, and my family I would need to create a large number of new miracles, but I was rested and more driven than ever. I executed my halfway house day job and worked five projects during the night and early mornings. And, as I used to say about sports, by a lot of hard work, and a great deal of fortune, we were able to create a process for paying the stakeholders, taking care of the family, and building for the future. I wanted to, eventually, give *60 Minutes* this incredible story of restoration for so many.

Then, on a random Tuesday, the BOP called me at work and ordered me to return home from my defense contractor job. I could not work there anymore. The explanation was nebulous. I submitted another BOP submission for another position, and it was rejected. I submitted a janitorial position with a downtown gym, but even this was rejected. On the thirtieth day, the BOP approved a new job instead of returning me to prison.

Based on this continuing debacle, the 55 Group, an aerospace manufacturer, offered to acquire more of my time and commitment. More providence. 55 Group proposed to the Department of Justice to pay $500,000 to *my victims* in return for transitioning me from home confinement to supervised release—a minor lifestyle change that allowed me to work even more for the company, my family, and my restitution recipients. The July 1, 2020, offer stated, "I write today on behalf of Mr. Martinovich to offer a payment of half a million dollars ($500,000.00) to be distributed to the individual victims pursuant to the restitution orders. The funds are in my firm trust account ready for immediate payment." I couldn't believe this offer of restoration for everyone.

USA Jessica Aber and AUSA Brian Samuels adamantly opposed the motions to provide this significant restoration. This incredibly rare gift was denied. Even the corporate attorneys were outraged. They could not believe the decisions to continually deny restitution and remedy. Wasn't this the purpose of the system? Judge Wright Allen had previously stated on the record it "would take a miracle" to pay back our stakeholders, but now, even a miracle would not work.

> Remember, when battling many forces you didn't even know existed, their objectives are likely not yours. You may think the solution to the adversity is *X*, but their objective may be *Y*. You should never assume knowledge of your adversaries' intents or objectives. I made this mistake, repeatedly, for years.

HOW COULD I HAVE ESCAPED IF I WAS AT HOME THE WHOLE TIME?

SERVING TIME UNDER HOME CONFINEMENT is certainly better than being in prison. But I can never forget there are two words in "home confinement" and the most important word is not "home."

While better than many alternatives, home confinement is still a very strange human existence. The constant anxiety of knowing my slightest misstep may return me to prison and the lack of control of movement and choices create daily physiological responses similar to full incarceration.

I am not allowed to leave my residence except for approved times to go directly to and from work, church, or an approved outing. Any exceptions have to be approved in advance. I call the halfway house when I leave the house and immediately when I get home. The telephone rings randomly four to five times each day and night. It's the halfway house calling to make sure I'm where I am supposed to be. If they don't hear my voice, bad things start to happen. I have fielded more than 4,000 such "accountability calls" since I was released to home confinement in May 2020.

The Halfway House Phoned

It started with one of those accountability calls. In the late evening of May 31, 2021, the halfway house dialed my house. I was in my bed asleep. But because the cable telephone system in the house went down at some point in the evening, the phone didn't ring. Okay, it was concerning, but there were multiple steps to determine if I was where I was supposed to be. Unfortunately for me, every one of those steps failed.

The best way to resolve the problem of unanswered phone calls is to send someone to the house for a *wellness check* so someone in authority can lay eyes on me. The halfway house requested that officers from the Norfolk Police Department come to the house and confirm that I was physically where I was supposed to be. At 11:22 p.m. two officers arrived at our door in Norfolk. So far, so good. But according to bodycam video and news reports, the officers "mistakenly believed they were coming to the halfway house itself." The officers chose not to ring the doorbell out of concern for waking up the residents. Instead, according to their own report, they lightly knocked. The house was dark. "Dude who runs [the halfway house] is probably asleep," said one of the officers, according to the report. Astounding! Neither Ashleigh nor I, nor the three Yorkshire Terriers, heard anyone at the door. The officers relayed to the halfway house that no one answered the door.

Even now the halfway house had a tool to confirm I was where I was supposed to be. The ankle monitor I was wearing is GPS-enabled so it can send an alarm when I go outside the perimeter of the house. On their screen, they could see the dot indicating the ankle monitor associated with me was stationery inside the house. According to the report the Bureau of Prisons would eventually produce, personnel at the halfway house confirmed this point.

Errors compounded. Another function of the ankle monitor is a vibration mechanism that can be activated remotely. With the push of a button, the halfway house can start the ankle bracelet vibrating to alert its wearer that his or her attention is required. The halfway house pushed the button three separate times. Alas, as the Bureau of Prisons in its written report later acknowledged, the vibration feature of my ankle monitor was inoperative.

Calm the Hysteria

At some point in the night, I awoke and discovered the halfway house had been trying to call me. I ran downstairs in a panic, called the halfway house, emailed everyone, and attempted to calm the mounting hysteria. I reported to the center, was advised this would be a one-time warning, and if I missed a phone call again, I would spend thirty days back at the halfway house. For a minute, I heaved a sigh of relief.

The Bureau of Prisons had a different idea and ignored the recommendations of my halfway house. The BOP charged me with ESCAPE 100, which for someone on home confinement was the most serious violation possible. The hedge fund shareholders, my victims, were all notified by email that I had escaped. On June 1, 2021, the US Marshalls arrived, cuffed me, shackled my legs, and took me back to prison, promising I would now, as an escapee, serve the remainder of my term (about seven years) at a high-security facility with other escapees and high-risk prisoners. The Bureau of Prisons had been aggressively clawing inmates accused of administrative violations back into prison. Critics of this policy had a name for this: "Getting back on budget."

I understood what was happening. The first goal of bureaucracies is self-perpetuation and increasing power. The Department of Justice and Bureau of Prisons are classic examples of bureaucracies that, naturally, work in their own self-interests. These organizations, just as with all others, perpetuate their interests to increase budgets, influence, and control. It was to be expected.

Ashleigh, for her part, six months pregnant and hysterical, was dazed that I, having never left her side, was now branded an escapee and taken away in chains by US Marshalls. She called Brian, Paul, and Kevin, and these Academy alumni brothers-in-arms, bless them, came to her side. My lifelong friends went immediately into battle mode, set up a virtual war room, and worked tirelessly for my release. They hired law firms, alerted the media, and gathered evidence and affidavits, to include police bodycam footage and officer reports documenting the myriad of misunderstandings.

Prison Tour

As for me, I got a new bird's-eye tour of a number of Bureau of Prisons facilities. I was shuttled between five different jails, starting in Virginia, through Oklahoma, and ending up in Mississippi. The administrative remedy paperwork could never keep up with my body, and the BOP administrators refused to return me home even though its own report confirmed the GPS data that I had never left my house and could not possibly have escaped.

The Cato Institute's *Reason Magazine* recounted my story in an October 2021 article titled "He Didn't Answer the Phone One Night While on House Arrest. He's Been Sent Back to Prison for Four Years."

Author Billy Binion wrote, "Government officials confirmed that the monitoring showed Martinovich was where he was supposed to be—his house. The device was not altered or messed with, per evidence from the FBP [Federal Bureau of Prisons]. But the agency proceeded with its conclusion regardless: He [Martinovich] had 'escape[d],' and thus deserves to spend years more behind bars after the government has already concluded he is not a threat to society. Such punitive measures do not make society any safer."

Emergency court motions were filed by Trey Kelleter, a Norfolk criminal defense attorney, who exhibited incredible compassion and commitment to uncover the truth and defend us. It was overwhelming to experience the team's efforts because for so long I had been the guilty-without-question prisoner who didn't deserve a voice. Just listening to someone else defend me brought my emotions to the breaking point behind bars.

I didn't know it at the time, but the tide changed in my favor. Maybe the heat of publicity aroused by this manifest injustice got too hot for the BOP. Things started to happen and of course no one explained any of it to me. Suddenly, I found myself in a Mississippi holding center. Then I heard that I was to be shuttled even further south to a high-security penitentiary. Unaware that the efforts on my behalf were gaining traction, I was afraid that I'd be locked away where no one could find me. I told the van driver that this was all a huge mistake! He didn't care.

As we drove up to the facility, the large gates opened, swirls of razor wire covered the high walls. Guards with automatic weapons surrounded our van. They led me into a holding cell, handed me an outfit consisting of Wrangler jeans and a white tee shirt. They put a plane ticket in my hand. A new shuttle driver, now a lot friendlier, dropped me off at the Jackson Mississippi International Airport and wished me luck. I was to find my way home, or somewhere, when sixty days ago I was a great danger to society.

Thoroughly rattled by my experience, I arrived in Norfolk. A very pregnant Ashleigh was waiting for me. Little baby Carleigh was due in two months. This time I didn't turn around for coffee mugs or anything else. Ashleigh and I hugged and cried and couldn't believe our current fortune, misfortune, or unbelievable life.

Sixty days had gone by since the Marshalls shackled me. How, I wondered, could my world change so quickly in two months. Adversity is the pain you never see coming.

KEEP THE FAITH, FINISH THE RACE

Life is not a journey to the grave with the intention of arriving safely in a well-preserved body, but rather to skid in broadside, thoroughly used up, totally worn out, and loudly proclaiming, "Wow what a ride!"

—HUNTER S. THOMPSON, THE PROUD HIGHWAY: SAGA OF A DESPERATE SOUTHERN GENTLEMAN

WELL, READER, WE HAVE COME TO THE END of this narrative and long list of lessons learned. I appreciate you taking this journey with me. Let's take final stock of the situation. As of this writing, I have been out of prison for a little more than three years. I remain in home confinement awaiting the official end of my sentence. My main goal is to be free of judicial restrictions so that I may kick the restoration project into high gear, for myself and so many others.

As you've learned through this narrative, my list of mistakes is nearly endless. I constantly distress over that damn company, EPV Solar. Over and over I play back in my mind the trip a few local CEOs and myself took to visit EPV's New Jersey manufacturing plant shortly before the meltdown. The plant was idled, awaiting a new round of orders as the executive team explained. The leaders on this visit initiated new distributor agreements with the company and even purchased more stock in EPV after this due diligence trip with the public-company management put in place for the upcoming IPO. But I should have been more skeptical, more thorough, as these business owners relied on me for advice and guidance. I failed to lead.

I'm constantly anguished over my immaturity to dismiss the regulators who knocked on our front door and went on what seemed a never-ending search for misdeeds. I failed to, right then and there, resolve these transgressions administratively and stop the escalation which not only killed the golden goose but also harmed so many employees and shareholders as a result. My dreadful business leadership is inexcusable.

> **Leaders addressing extreme adversity fall victim to what Adam Grant terms** *escalation of commitment.* **Due to our ego, sunk cost in our decisions, and identity with our position power, we often double-down on bad decisions instead of fixing the problem when the crisis is still manageable.**

Tentacles of Disaster

The tentacles of this disaster still reach into my daily activities. I live with five check-in phone calls. The BOP controls my work and controls my modest finances. I live in constant fear that someone using this control may hurt my family and myself. I live in the shadow of my *Google factor.* Just search my name and you will know what I mean. Mostly I live with constant guilt for all the mistakes I must make up for. But every day I make just a little more progress pushing these fears to side, brain compartmentalizing, and rebuilding confidence, compassion, and inspiration.

> The scars of extreme adversity can run deep but think of them as reminders to live our best lives forward. Scars can add wisdom and perspective, and they can encourage us to focus on the big picture and not spend our lives in the minutia of mere existence. They can be our gift.

I am constantly asked, "Would you make the same decisions again? Would you still reject the plea offers and stand up for what you believed was right?"

I always answer affirmatively that I would, and although we never truly know these answers until we are facing the fire, I still think these were, for me, the correct answers. I don't believe we came down to the planet this time around to seek the most comfortable existence. I imagine we are meant to struggle, grow, achieve, and overcome, and this is our journey, our reason for living. Sure, life can be enjoyable when everything is going our way, but I don't think that is why we go to all the trouble of attempting the human experience.

Hope and Inspiration

Most mornings I wake at 5:30 a.m., tiptoe up the stairs to my home office to start my long list of projects, and take a few quiet moments to thank the mysterious universe for my survival, but mostly for the incredible miracles I cannot explain.

My family, work, close friends, and numerous new missions give my days and weeks incredible hope and inspiration to make this next chapter of my life an even more exciting journey.

I'm also often asked, "What is the greatest lesson I've learned from this odyssey?"

When I was twenty-nine years old, doctors told me I had cancer. My therapy included immediate surgery and then an intense radiation program. Through that battle, and for many years after, I said a morning prayer of appreciation for everyone and everything. I wanted to hold onto that *cancer-scare feeling* to understand just how precious every day truly was. In that sense, cancer was a gift. Then somewhere along the way, as with so many things, I let the prayers fade. I forgot the intense appreciation of every single day. Well, now through this whole journey I've shared with you, I've been given another gift.

I hated every second of prison, but I remember also not enjoying nearly every second of my four years at the Air Force Academy. My father would constantly advise, "Afterwards, you will be extremely proud you made it through." And, of course, my father was right.

In a similar, mysterious way, I am extremely proud of making it through this horrific challenge and beginning to experience *the other end of the tunnel.* I often borrow Malcolm Gladwell's stories of turning disadvantages into advantages as I believe he has rightly focused on the locus of character. I pray I will be worthy of these narratives and be able to keep the faith and finish the race.

I keep telling Ashleigh I am looking forward to one day laughing, singing, and even dancing, again. Not in my fake, self-coached, exterior-armor-way, but to really let my guard down, be vulnerable, and feel like it's okay—without neither guilt nor remorse, but in acceptance of what the poet Mary Oliver calls "your one wild and precious life."

> The pressure of leadership and continual achievement often causes us to reach a point at which we fear losing more than we enjoy winning. This is the point when great coaches suddenly retire or exit the game without warning. We cannot find enjoyment and we've forgotten why we started this journey in the first place. We understand we must regain our passion, and this becomes a full-time mission when attempting to fully overcome extreme adversity.

And, again, my friends always ask me how I snagged such a beautiful woman as Ashleigh. My standard answer is, "I can't explain it. The universe works in mysterious ways, so I'm just going with it!" This encapsulates my philosophy for the next chapter of my life. Maybe it's my last chapter, and maybe—God only knows—it's the first chapter of a new book whose ending is anyone's guess. I now, finally, understand the meaning of the Old Yiddish proverb *Mann Tracht, Un Gott Lacht*. Man Plans, and God Laughs.

All I can do these days is to wake up early every morning, give it a hellacious effort of positivity and strength, and see what results occur. There is a startling freedom in believing we don't really control the outcomes.

Restitution, Restoration

One of my many commitments under this restoration project is to pay back all those who lost money due to my mistakes and failing to keep my eyes on the prize. I am committed to doing so not just because restitution is legally required, but because it is the right thing to do. I feel terrible that a lot of innocent people who put their faith in me lost money.

I am focused on attacking every day thinking in abundance, not scarcity. I recently moved our extended family into our urban neighborhood, which I call *the bubble*, and we have all reestablished bonds and made new strong relationships. I am enjoying my miraculous family, my incredible business opportunities, and the gift of being able to help so many others prevent and overcome their own challenges. The work is more rewarding than I ever could have imagined.

> **Leaders overcoming adversity should make it a habit to regularly read the *Wall Street Journal* obituary section and note two consistent themes: ordinary people with humble beginnings create fascinating lives with accomplishments never imagined, and most every life story has a hardship, a tragedy, which undoubtedly provided the character and strength to enable this great person to lead this enviable life.**

I've always believed great leaders study the world and learn from others' mistakes instead of having to learn from their own experiences, so I believe my final mission is to help so many others study my failures:

- *While building the successful company and reputation, I could have put in place so many protections and safety nets to, later, survive multiple black swans.*

- *I should have kept my powder dry to absorb bad decisions, bad economies, and significant shifts in the regulatory environment.*

- *I should have replaced our private shareholders to protect them from my poor decisions.*

- *I should have replaced all my family's personal guarantees once the company had grown to its independent station.*

- *I should have protected the different companies and services from each other in order to stop a domino effect from my mistakes.*

- *I should not have allowed individuals to invest such a high percentage of their futures in the success of MICG, both clients and employees.*

- *Based on the experiences of my own life, I should have understood success is not a continuous, straight-line slope.*

- *I should have taken some chips off the table and put them away for a rainy day.*

- *I should not have let the rewards of success make me softer and less focused.*

- *After twenty years of outworking everyone, I should have handed the reins to someone else and enjoyed the rewards without jeopardizing the success of so many.*

- *I should have stayed the captain and not the coach, providing daily leadership-by-example, not telling others to overachieve on their own.*

- *I should not have handed the Ferrari keys to the valet in front of the small-town theater just so I felt important.*

- *At some point, I should have reasoned with the chip-on-the-shoulder 5'9" D1 point guard inside my mind and taught him to compromise, accept a few losses, and live for another day, for everyone's sake.*

But even with the hundreds of mistakes laid bare for the reader in this narrative, I have come through this challenge with miracles, blessings, and providence, which could have never been imagined. I am healthy, happy, and focused on building another mission of significance. I, now, only work on projects in which I believe I can provide a tremendous impact, and I only work with people I love.

My family is thriving, I am making progress on restoration for so many, and I believe this journey has made me wiser, stronger, and more compassionate. My new morning prayer asks the universe to help me make the right decisions today, to spread love and compassion, and to give others hope and inspiration. This is my mission.

I am an incredibly lucky man. I wish each of you tremendous success. Be the class and grace leader you know you were meant to be. Keep speaking victory.

SUMMARY OF LESSONS, TAKEAWAYS, AND BEST PRACTICES

This chapter collects in one place all the lessons, takeaways, and best practices introduced in the previous chapters. The lessons are presented here in the same order they are presented in the book.

On Avoiding Overconfidence. When adversity shows up on our doorstep, we have to instantly realize we don't know what we don't know. My biggest mistakes, at the most critical moments, came from my overconfidence in believing I was smart enough to navigate these treacherous waters. I should have accepted that this game had a completely different set of rules. I should have, also, allowed my planning and strategy to be open to terrible outcomes and possibilities I dreaded. In a sense, my overconfidence and previous success blinded me to the fact there was an extremely high probability that the battle I was fighting was already lost.

On the Nature of Adversity. Adversity comes unexpectedly and there's often nothing you can do to prevent it. All you can do is cultivate resilience, remember you are never alone, and pivot.

On Accepting Responsibility. When faced with adversity, great leaders must take the responsibility to make good on the contract entrusted to us by our employees, shareholders, and family. We have to perform at these most critical moments, put the interests of our beneficiaries ahead of our own, and do whatever it takes to lead those put in our charge to calmer waters.

On Controlling One's Destiny. I made a vow to never again put myself in a position where my destiny depended on someone else.

On Practicing Daily Productive Actions. Overcoming great adversity requires pragmatic, solutions-oriented efforts applied over and over until achieving final victory. More times than not, the paths we feel will be productive are not, and the outlier efforts in which we had little faith come through for us. Therefore, daily, exhaustive, productive actions are mandatory in order to even have a chance at survival. Failure is not an option.

On Practicing Humility. If we have the foresight to arrange our lives today not only in preparation for continued success but also in anticipation of extreme adversity that will likely appear, our chances of survival will increase dramatically. If I had practiced greater humility in my material acquisitions, as well as my lifestyle and personal choices, I would have likely fared much better in my challenges with regulators, shareholders, and jurors.

On Purging Sycophants. One advantage of going through severe adversity for CEOs and other leaders is the purging of the sycophants who have told us what we wanted to hear and empowered our reckless or out-of-touch decision-making. It's not difficult to recognize the flatterers. Look for the followers that laugh loudest at the feeble jokes we tell. CEOs as a rule are really not that funny.

On Not Being Sure of Intentions and Objectives of Others. Remember, when battling many forces you didn't even know existed, their objectives are likely not yours. You may think the solution to the adversity is *X*, but their objective may be *Y*. You should never assume knowledge of your adversaries' intents or objectives. I made this mistake, repeatedly, for years.

A Tip for Overcoming Extreme Adversity. Write down a list of all the people, places, and things you have been fortunate to experience in your incredible life. Then write a new bucket list of the amazing things you will accomplish once you figure out how to get outside the other end of this tunnel.

On the Imperative for Physical Fitness. I understood the necessity of religiously committing to physical strength and fitness every single day. It was not an option, but mandatory. Whether part of our life already or a foreign practice, once the black swan shows up on a random Tuesday, we must dive into health and strength immediately in order to survive.

***

On the Imperative of Intellectual Development. I realized I must immerse myself in intellectual development and education in order to control my own destiny. I could not rely on attorneys, accountants, or industry experts to have the knowledge. I would have to find intellectual paths less traveled to be victorious.

***

On Committing to Something Greater Than Oneself. When massive adversity occurs, such as the government knocks on our office door, or an unexpected event uproots and attempts to destroy our successful life, we have to commit to something greater than ourselves. That's the essence of religion, whatever that may be for each of us. That something greater exists gives us hope there can be a better life than what we have right now. Short fights, sprints, are possible through sheer will, but wars, marathons, require a belief in something deep, deep down in our souls.

***

On Never Volunteering. Never volunteer, offer information, or get involved willingly with the individuals and organizations charged to monitor, regulate, or penalize you. I facilitated them finding a case where there was no case to begin with. My foolish actions to volunteer, likely stemming from narcissistic desires to be important in our industry, served up our demise on a silver platter.

On Understanding That Everyone Is Vulnerable. This realization came too late for me to understand the fundamental adversity risk to every successful CEO and entrepreneur: If they enter your business, it is impossible for them to not uncover a long list of violations, and even felonies, with which they may choose to indict you.

On There Being No Handbook to Adversity. At times of extreme adversity, no one gives us a handbook on how to properly conduct ourselves. Every day and issue are new challenges we never expected to face, but if we can push fear to the side, and draw upon our years of development and training, we can, hopefully, make more good choices than bad. But this is only for us to understand, and we cannot seek others to grasp our motives or approve of our decisions.

On Fighting the Battle Early. Fight your battle early. If you appease the black swan instead of confronting it and standing up for what you believe is right, it can rapidly expand into an overwhelming and unmanageable, even existential, challenge. Be Churchill, not Chamberlain.

On Communicating Your Own Narrative. Perception is reality, and vacuums will be filled by your opponents if you do not act quickly and decisively to control the information. If you don't control your narrative, your adversaries will. Remember the wisdom of Gordon Gekko in *Wall Street*: "The most valuable commodity I know of is information."

On Being Tested by Adversity. Leaders understand they will be tested by adversity. Success rarely comes easily and when it does there is every risk it will eventually disappear. Leaders understand that success must be earned and it cannot arrive without patience and struggle. Nothing is more fragile than success that appears effortless.

On Making Decisions with Confidence. Overcoming extreme adversity often demands we make one or multiple pivotal decisions. Yet, if throughout our life we take on challenges others shy away from, and we build as much character and positive success in our memory bank as possible, we may have enough courage to make that truly existential decision we always hoped we could handle. These prior training grounds give us the confidence and energy to be the leader we always hoped we could be.

On Helping Others. Help as many people as possible, and the universe will, in turn, reward you with results and victories far beyond what you, and everyone else, believed was possible. It is a mathematical truism. It was the law of attraction before I even knew the meaning of the phrase.

On Creating a New Rolodex. I reminded myself daily to help as many people as possible, in the knowledge that this approach was my only chance to help myself. When faced with extreme adversity, we must accept that our previous database, our previous life, will likely be erased, but a new database is always available for construction.

On Accepting That Wealth May Not Save Us. When faced with extreme adversity, even ones that may take our liberty, we have to understand the wealth we built over all these years may have little impact on our likelihood of success, or even survival. Our money cannot free us. Even the most powerful, connected CEO must pivot and return to relying on their own abilities and the goodwill developed by helping others.

On the Power of Integrity. When considering integrity, a leader will likely identify with the definition of "the quality of being honest and having strong moral principles." Yet when facing extreme adversity, leaders should consider the secondary definition as "the state of being whole and undivided." Character and integrity many times are no match for resourceful adversaries who may align multiple estates in unison. Leaders must prepare to combat their adversity on multiple fronts, simultaneously, in order to navigate a path to victory.

On Taking Inventory of Vulnerabilities. How many CEOs and entrepreneurs reading this are right now taking inventory of what will be turned against them once extreme adversity arrives?

On Caring for Others. Extreme adversity so clearly highlights the demarcation line many times between caring for ourselves and making sure our employees, or even our children, are going to be okay. If we have invested great time, energy, and resources into their knowledge, attitudes, and overachieving culture, they will grow up to be fine without us. Our finest achievement is for them *not* to need us, especially when we make the incredible mistakes I have.

On Preparing for the Worst. Policies, protocols, and people need to be set with a view to prepare for the worst that could happen. Hope is not a strategy. Blind optimism is not a strategy. I urge all leaders to reassess their own vulnerability in the same manner the US military constantly war games scenario after scenario of terrible events befalling the country.

On Avoiding Self-Pity. As leaders confronted with extreme adversity, we must aspire to more. We must throw aside all excuses of "this is not fair" or "they owe me because I have been so successful." The forces may align against us with overwhelming strength and control, but we must *play the cards we are dealt.* To rage against the system, or the universe, only furthers our decline into self-pity and victimhood. This guarantees defeat. We must accept what we feel is wrong and unfair and focus all our energy and intellect on overcoming what, to us, feels greatly unjust.

On Not Succumbing to Despair. Sometimes adversity can require extreme humility and basic survival instincts just to be able to remain alive long enough to find a path to victory. As crazy as it may sound during comfortable times, first focusing on staying alive may become the primary objective without which nothing else is possible. Mentally and physically, we must become as clever and strong as possible to not take our own lives, as a number of my associates had in the wake of the 2008 Financial Crisis, and to not let violence, disease, or fatal maladies destroy us before we are able to rise from the ashes.

On Preparing to Win. Our company's focus on etiquette, character, class, proper human behavior, and superior knowledge created a fundamental base that later, in extreme adversity, positioned me to operate in adverse elements and better navigate the challenges confronting me. I believe with basketball coach Bobby Knight that "Most people have the will to win, few have the will to prepare to win."

On Appreciation and Gratitude. Even though earlier I described how we are all alone with the responsibility to save ourselves when extreme adversity strikes, there are also times when we cannot let our hearts be so hardened, and our plates of armor so impenetrable, that we miss a gift that reminds us we are not alone. All the answers are inside us if we are only quiet enough to listen. Ashleigh is a gift, a miracle, and I have spent each day since receiving that letter determined to honor her and make her life a miracle, also.

On Balancing Cynicism and Optimism. When battling entrenched adversaries, we must find a delicate balance between cynicism to protect ourselves and humility and optimism to give us the energy to keep going. As exhausting as it may be, we must keep our radar on high intensity to see around corners or otherwise we will be vulnerable to unseen attacks. As strong leaders, we can reestablish our vulnerability and kindness once the threat has passed.

On Becoming Self-Aware. When thrown into extreme adversity, we must, first, understand we don't know what we don't know, and commit to 1) realizing our mistakes, 2) instantly becoming more self-aware and educated about our new problem, and 3) mitigate mistakes as quickly as possible to counter the natural progression toward compounding and escalating complications.

On Not Relying on Others. To emphasize one more time, through extreme adversity become a master of whatever business you must handle. Never, ever, ever rely on attorneys, accountants, or bankers to do the work you should be doing yourself. They must preserve their own existence and will only go so far in uncovering your truths or standing up for your rights. You must control your destiny.

On the Necessity of Compartmentalization. Extreme adversity brings what seems like a never-ending flow of crisis after crisis, each with seemingly more intense ramifications. Compartmentalization, the ability to shift *this list* of traumatic problems to one side and use the other side of the brain to refocus on the new dramas right in front of us, is a critical skill for survival.

On the Necessity to Document Everything. Even before the black swan knocks on our doors, we must, sadly, document everything possible to include paperwork, audio recordings, and even video interviews. It saved my life, over and over, during this horrific decade, but I should have implemented this extreme practice twenty years earlier.

Today, my consulting associates chuckle when I demand that every contract or disclaimer signing be videotaped.

On the Benefits of Shifting Your Perspective. When you confront conditions you neither chose nor can readily manage, it is helpful to shift your perspective. That shift can take many forms. But the common element is by thinking or doing something differently to change yourself or your situation. Shifting one's perspective expands the imagination, increases focus, and streamlines the main goal of leaders: to find clarity.

On Demanding Complete Information. Organizational hierarchies prevent leaders from getting essential truths and candid opinions, especially if they contradict opinions contrary to what followers think the leader wants to hear. We struggle because we get told only a portion of what we need to know. We have to demand, "Look, I need to hear what I'm missing. Tell me what you're not telling me." And then we must listen and, most importantly, never punish or ostracize bearers of bad news.

On Occasionally Being Ruthless. I had to take to heart one more piece of advice from Nassim Taleb's *Black Swan: The Impact of the Highly Improbable*, "You can afford to be compassionate, lax, and courteous if, once in a while, when it is least expected of you, but completely justified, you sue someone, or savage an enemy, just to show that you can walk the walk."

On Serving Others. Here's a truth demonstrated repeatedly through history: when people experience extreme adversity but focus on helping others instead of themselves, the human spirit is energized and begins to heal itself. Serving others is a gift that rebounds to the gift-giver. The practice represents the most potent medicine to avoid despair and self-pity while regaining one's own strength and self-confidence.

On Understanding Public Opinion. When facing great adversity, the high-profile leader must understand that public opinion and *system opinion* will likely be entrenched against them. Leaders must realize their efforts, arguments, remedies, and solutions must be far beyond what they would previously have found proportionate and equitable. Leaders must accept, and commit to, giving outsized efforts many times greater than everyone else in order to achieve a survivable, or, better yet, victorious, solution.

On Turning the Tide. In extreme adversity, the waterfall seems to gain more force and velocity against you in a never-ending current. Then one day, sometimes imperceptibly, the tide starts to turn. Getting to the camp, winning a couple of reversals, removing the latest impediment to justice. And then you gain momentum, compound your victories, begin to turn the tide of power, and even begin to take control of the narrative. Joel Osteen said, "We don't have to win, sometimes we just have to outlast them."

On Recognizing Small Successes. When committed to overcoming extreme adversity, once the tide begins to turn we can, literally, feel momentum building in our favor. Just as a PGA golfer feels his swing suddenly hit the right groove, and week after week he surprises the field with multiple victories, we have to take advantage of this break in the storm. We see sun rays streaming through the storm clouds, and we have to redouble our efforts and begin to change our angle of effort from just merely surviving to, possibly, winning and thriving.

On Saying "Yes" to Opportunities. When battling for survival, we must take advantage of every opportunity life presents us, even if the window is only slightly cracked open and it is impossible to connect the dots to an eventual benefit. Just as in business where we must constantly train ourselves to say "yes" to the smallest invitations, which may turn into great successes, in adversity we must fight the natural inclinations of pessimism, hopelessness, and not *swinging at every pitch*. It was always the motions, the arguments, and the changes which I never thought would make a difference that helped me blindly navigate my way to survival and restoration.

On Reckoning with the Costs Adversity Imposes. Leaders need to be honest with themselves that great adversity takes a toll on their physical and mental health, as well as the soul, and that repair time will be necessary. Fortunately, great leaders are normally not the types who wallow in this misery but that have great strength and experience to rebound from failure, lick their wounds, and charge forward. We simply need to acknowledge this serious step in the process.

On Accepting the Inevitability of Roadblocks. Recovery from extreme adversity and failure happens in *fits and spurts*. We must become comfortable living with roadblocks at every turn. Just when we feel we are making progress, the phone will ring, or the summons will appear, and we are back in fight-or-flight mode. We have to stay focused and realize it remains a long journey and not let recurring adversity break our spirit for ultimate recovery.

Jeff Martinovich

Jeff Martinovich earned his BS in Business Management from the US Air Force Academy and his MBA in Finance from The College of William and Mary. He had the honor of serving his country during The First Gulf War at Tactical Air Command Headquarters, Langley, Virginia. Pursuing a second career in financial services, Jeff was founder and CEO of MICG Investment Management, a billion-dollar wealth management firm nationally recognized for its rapid growth, wow service, and A-Player culture. Following the 2008 Financial Crisis, MICG's proprietary hedge funds experienced regulatory scrutiny and allegations, resulting in Jeff being sentenced to fourteen years in federal prison. And here begins the rest of the story. More recently Jeff spends his busy days growing companies, speaking to leadership organizations, and appreciating every second with Ashleigh, Cole, and Carleigh. He lives in Norfolk, Virginia.

John Kador

John Kador is the author of over twenty-five books including *What Every Angel Investor Wants You to Know, Charles Schwab: How One Company Beat Wall Street and Reinvented the Brokerage Industry*, and *Effective Apology: Building Bridges and Restoring Trust.* John graduated from Duke University with a BA in English, received a Master's degree in public relations from The American University, and is a contributing editor at *Wealth Management Magazine*. He lives with his wife in Winfield, Pennsylvania.

ACKNOWLEDGMENTS

Thank You

To John Kador, an incredible writer, for believing in me and giving me the courage to tackle this overwhelming project with him. Thank you for your wisdom, kindness, and friendship.

To Brian Raduenz for almost single-handedly making my restoration and next business chapters possible. To Paul Meyer for teaching me *putting the band back together* is one of the most rewarding projects a man can undertake. To Kevin Cadieux for proving loyalty and being there for one another through the good and the bad are the promises of best friends.

To Colonel Ray Valas for his literary wisdom, strength, and patriotism. To Jeffery Clevenger for investing incredible time in my writings and compelling me to keep getting better. To Trey Kelleter for coming to get me when all seemed lost, again. To Nat Pierce for looking out for me and trusting me in business and friendship.

To my Forbes Books publishing team of Patti, Caroline, Beth, Steve, Analisa, and so many great supporters, thank you.

To Ashleigh for being the most gorgeous person I've ever known, inside and out. To Cole for forgiving me for all my mistakes and giving me the opportunity to work side by side with an amazing son, every day. To little Carleigh for bringing such joy into our family and forcing me to be strong for another twenty years! To Linda and Bill for adopting me into the family. And, finally, to my incredible mother, Charlene, for every day proving optimism attracts the world, and my amazing father, Don, who even though his father had left him, taught me strength, courage, and the importance of having a supportive, never-failing father.

CONTACT THE AUTHOR

Jeff Martinovich, an exciting and accomplished speaker and educator, is passionate about helping leaders not make the same mistakes he made, as well as reforming and restoring our great nation.

Jeff provides engaging keynote addresses, corporate panels and workshops, and one-on-one advisory to business leaders and individuals focused on protecting success on the way up, or managing adverse situations on the way down, with the benefits of his experience.

If you would like to follow Jeff's writings and events, or contact him for a speaking engagement with your company or organization, please reach out to the following:

https://jeffmartinovich.com/

https://www.facebook.com/jeffrey.martinovich.1/

https://www.linkedin.com/in/jeff-martinovich/

https://www.instagram.com/jeffmartinovich/

https://twitter.com/JeffMartinovich

https://www.youtube.com/channel/UCpLIvBIfotBiHSuPAZE3woA

jam@jeffmartinovich.com

FINANCIAL INDUSTRY REGULATORY AUTHORITY

OFFICE OF HEARING OFFICERS

Department of Enforcement,
 	
      Complainant,
 	
v.
 	
MICG Investment Management, LLC
CRD No. 104028,
 	
and
 	
Jeffrey A. Martinovich
CRD No. 2258793,
 	
      Respondents.
	DISCIPLINARY PROCEEDING
	No. 2009016230501
	
	Hearing Officer: MC

OFFER OF SETTLEMENT

I.

Respondents MICG Investment Management, LLC (MICG) and Jeffrey A. Martinovich (Martinovich) (collectively, Respondents) make this Offer of Settlement (Offer) to the Financial Industry Regulatory Authority (FINRA), with respect to the matters alleged by FINRA in Disciplinary Proceeding No. 2009016230501 filed on May 14, 2010 (Complaint).

Respondents submit this offer to resolve this proceeding and do not admit or deny the allegations of the Complaint. Respondents also submit this offer upon the condition that FINRA shall not institute or entertain, at any time, any further proceeding as to Respondents based on the allegations of the Complaint, and upon further condition that it will not be used in this proceeding, in any other proceeding, or otherwise, unless it is accepted by the National Adjudicatory Council (NAC) Review Subcommittee, pursuant to FINRA Rule 9270.

21

FILED
IN OPEN COURT

FEB 1 0 2016

CLERK, U.S. DISTRICT COURT
NEWPORT NEWS, VA

IN THE UNITED STATES DISTRICT COURT FOR THE
EASTERN DISTRICT OF VIRGINIA
Newport News Division

UNITED STATES OF AMERICA	)	CRIMINAL. NO. 4:15cr50
	)	
v.	)	18 U.S.C. §§ 1341 and 2
	)	Mail Fraud
JEFFREY A. MARTINOVICH,	)	(Count One)
	)	
Defendant.	)	18 U.S.C. §§ 1343 and 2
	)	Wire Fraud
	)	(Count Two)
	)	
	)	18 U.S.C. §§ 1957 and 2
	)	Engaging in Monetary Transactions in
	)	Property Derived from Specified Unlawful
	)	Activity
	)	(Count Three)
	)	
	)	18 U.S.C. §§ 1956(a)(1)(B)(i) and 2
	)	Concealment Money Laundering
	)	(Counts Four through Thirteen)

SUPERSEDING INDICTMENT

February 2016 Term - At Newport News, Virginia

GENERAL ALLEGATIONS

1.   In or about 1999, JEFFREY A. MARTINOVICH (hereinafter "MARTINOVICH"),
the defendant herein, formed Martinovich Investment Consulting Group ("MICG"), a financial
services company that offered investment advice and other investment-related services to clients.
MICG was headquartered in Newport News, Virginia, within the Eastern District of Virginia.

2.   MICG utilized the services of First Clearing, LLC, ("First Clearing") a non-bank
affiliate of Wells Fargo & Company (a financial institution as defined under 18 U.S.C. § 20), to
provide brokerage account services, including the compilation and issuance of investor statements
with account and/or investment portfolio information.   Such statements were sent to investors by

1

UNITED STATES DISTRICT COURT
FOR THE EASTERN DISTRICT COURT OF VIRGINIA

JEFFREY A. MARTINOVICH,
    Petitioner,

  v.

UNITED STATES,
    Respondent.

Case No. 4:2018cv00027
Case No. 4:2018cv00028

(4:12cr101)
(4:15cr50)

MOTION FOR CURRENT MEDIATION AND SETTLEMENT IN FAVOR OF MICG
SHAREHOLDERS AND ELIMINATION OF FURTHER SIGNIFICANT EXPENDITURE OF
GOVERNMENT RESOURCES AND TAXPAYER EXPENSE PURUSUANT TO
28 U.S.C. § 651 AND LOCAL RULE 83.6

NOW HERE COMES Jeffrey A. Martinovich, proceeding pro se, in a
Motion for Current Mediation and Settlement in Favor of MICG Shareholders
and Elimination of Further Significant Expenditure of Government
Resources and Taxpayer Expense Pursuant to 28 U.S.C. § 651 and Local
Rule 83.6. The Fourth Circuit has stated that "the § 2255 remedy is
broad and flexible, and entrusts to the courts the power to fashion
an appropriate remedy." [U.S. v. Hadden, 475 3d 652 (4th Cir. 2006).

"Congress finds that alternative dispute resolution, including
mediation, may provide greater efficiency in achieving settlements
and reduce the large backlog of cases now pending in Federal Courts"
in order to aid MICG Shareholders now. [28 USC § 651, PL 105-315 § 2,
112 Stat. 2993]. Mr. Martinovich respectfully submits to this Honorable
Court the documentation of previous attempts to resolve this legal
challenge in favor of restoring the shareholders of MICG Inv. Mgt.,
and in-turn reduce the future significant time and expense of the
Court and the United States in continuing litigation. Said efforts
have attempted to restore the noted investors and victims pursuant
to the Government demands as well as likely go much further beyond
Government requests in Case 4:12cr101 and 4:15cr50 in fully restoring

1

THE UNITED STATES DISTRICT COURT
IN THE EASTERN DISTRICT OF VIRGINIA

UNITED STATES,

    Plaintiff,

v.

Case No. 4:12cr101

JEFFREY A. MARTINOVICH,

    Defendant.

MEMORANDUM IN SUPPORT OF MOTION TO VACATE, SET ASIDE,
OR CORRECT A SENTENCE PURSUANT TO 28 U.S.C. § 2255

NOW HERE COMES Jeffrey A. Martinovich, proceeding pro se, in a Motion to Vacate, Set Aside, or Correct a Sentence Pursuant to 28 U.S.C. § 2255.

LEGAL STANDARD

"The United States Supreme Court holds allegations of a pro se complaint to less stringent standards than formal pleadings drafted by lawyers. A complaint should not be dismissed for failure to state a claim unless it appears beyond doubt that the plaintiff can prove no set of facts in support of his claim which would entitle him relief." [Haines v. Kerner, 404 U.S. 519, 520-21, 92 S. Ct. 594, 30 L. Ed 2d 652 (1972)].

Mr. Martinovich presents this Motion pursuant to 28 U.S.C. § 2255(a) which permits that "(a) prisoner in custody under sentence of a court established by Act of Congress claiming the right to be released upon the ground that the sentence was imposed in violation of the Constitution or laws of the United

1

IN THE UNITED STATES DISTRICT COURT
FOR THE EASTERN DISTRICT OF VIRGINIA

JEFFREY A. MARTINOVICH,   )
    Petitioner,   )   Case Nos. 4:15cr50/4:18cv27
)
)
v.   )   Honorable Chief Judge Mark S. Davis
)
)
UNITED STATES,   )
    Respondent   )

MOTION TO RESCIND AND WITHDRAWAL PETITIONER'S MOTION TO VACATE, SET ASIDE, OR CORRECT A SENTENCE PURSUANT TO 28 U.S.C. SEC. 2255

NOW HERE COMES Jeffrey A. Martinovich, proceeding pro se and in forma pauperis, in a Motion and Notice to respectfully request this Honorable Court Grant Rescission and Withdrawal of Petitioner's Motion to Vacate, Set Aside, or Correct a Sentence Pursuant to 28 U.S.C. Sec. 2255, and any and all collateral appeals and Hearings.

NOTICE TO WITHDRAWAL

Mr. Martinovich, by another miracle, has recently discovered that he will soon be a father, again, with a due date of September 13, 2021. Based on the unexpected and before thought implausible outcomes of his trial proceedings, reversals, violent incarceration, confidential proceedings, and re-sentencings, Mr. Martinovich cannot now afford to continue his pursuit of truth and restoration of stakeholders.

When Mr. Martinovich, along with his attorneys' concurrence, rejected three Government plea offers in pursuit of the truth and ability to re-establish his shareholders, his only son was entering college, was fully prepared for the world, and was consulted in this decision. Now, Mr. Martinovich does not have the luxury to defend himself and fight for the current restoration of his stakeholders. The possible and potentially extraordinary outcomes of further proceedings

1

ENDNOTES

1   Government response to petitioner's motion for compassionate release and/or in the alternative for sentence reduction or reduction to time served pursuant to 28 USC SEC 2255 in support of all stakeholders' objectives.

2   Memorandum in support of motion to vacate, set aside, or correct a sentence pursuant to 28 USC § 225.

INDEX

Y

Young Presidents' Organization (YPO), 12

www.ingramcontent.com/pod-product-compliance
Lightning Source LLC
Chambersburg PA
CBHW031502180326
41458CB00044B/6669/J